YORKIES HEAD TO TAIL

THE ESSENTIAL CARE GUIDE

YORKIES HEAD TO TAIL

THE ESSENTIAL CARE GUIDE

Sandra Lemire

Paper Chase Press
New Orleans, LA

NOTICE: This book is intended to be a reference volume only, not a medical manual. The information contained within is designed to help you make informed decisions about your pet's health. It is not intended as a substitute for any treatment prescribed by your veterinarian. The author urges that if your pet has a medical problem, you take the information gained herein and seek competent medical assistance.

"Candy's Story," by Kris Dickinson (chapter 1), used with permission.

"A Report from the Drill Instructor of an Ex-Yappy Little Dog," by Amy Tan, reprinted from *The New Yorkie Times* with permission.

"Lobo's Story," used with permission.

"Rainbow Bridge Return," by Joy LaCaille (lakai@iag.net), used with permission.

Paper Chase Press books may be purchased for educational, business or sales promotional use. For information, please write: Special Markets Department, Paper Chase Press, 5721 Magazine Street, New Orleans, LA 70115.

FIRST EDITION

ISBN: 1-879706-83-0
LC: 99-075876
Printed in the USA.

Cover photo: dog on left, © Dale Churchill, 1999; dog on right, © Jennifer Osborn, 1999

Illustrations by Gail DeLay.

Dedication

I want to send a message with this work that we as women can do everything and anything we can envision. There are no limits as long as we don't set any for ourselves. My mother, Dayne Colleen was a pioneer for women, as was her mother, my grandmother, Loree. From being the first woman to be a licensed CPA in the state of Nevada, to my grandmother being an airplane mechanic during World War II, these women always set goals above and beyond the realm of what was expected or accepted for women.

Both of these women had faith in me and passed their torch to me to push myself beyond my own limits. I wish they had lived long enough to see my books published, but I know their spirits continue to push me further. They are with me in my heart and a bright light in my memory.

ACKNOWLEDGMENTS

There are many comrades and companions who have walked my path with me toward the good that this book might inspire. I must thank Gary Corey who continues to make all things possible, even the impossible. I need to convey my deepest respect and regard for the genius and talent of Isabel Molina of RingWise. Her support and encouragement during a time when caring for her son Daniel became her life calling have been invaluable. I appreciate to no end the faith and support of Anita Kitchens, whose work toward education and reaching out is immeasurable.

In view of an automobile accident that occurred shortly after starting work on this project and created major setbacks in my progress, I owe a great debt of gratitude to my editor, Jennifer Osborn. She remained steadfast, organized, dedicated and patient throughout this project.

My greatest tribute and appreciation for all good things that might emanate from this writing goes to the veterinarians who have opened their minds and their wealth of knowledge to me and so many breeders and pet lovers that have reached out for their help. These vets came to my home to help with dehydrating calves, ecclampsia, post-delivery check-ups, tail docking, vaccinations, letting go, artificial inseminations, and more. They worked with me by telephone across the nation to help bitches in life-threatening situations. They trusted my instincts when there was no proof that I was right or wrong. They put their egos aside to work side by side, letting me participate the best way I could. They were willing to learn and even ask my advice if they thought it would make a difference to a patient. Some of these vets were for my own animals and others were strangers who took a chance and believed in me for the treatment of other people's animals that were in desperate need. These vets are indeed true healers and doctors in the essence of the word, meaning "teachers."

Table of Contents

Introduction

"It's not the money. It never has been. I've lost a fortune in Yorkies."

Seventeen years ago I was raising my family when I fell in love with Yorkshire Terriers and decided I wanted to become a credible breeder. I wanted to participate in the miracle of birth, to raise and maybe show these delightful little dogs and to breed in all those wonderful traits that make Yorkies so captivating. I had no illusions about my place in the general order of things and had long since given up the notion that I would make a difference in the world. I just wanted to breed Yorkies.

Before I turned to Yorkies, I was involved in raising horses, cattle, chickens and other barnyard animals. I soon discovered that most farmers live by statistics and their decisions have to be based on the bottom line. When a house call for a sick calf ran $100, including antibiotics and electrolytes, but the calf was only worth $100, I did some fast learning about caring for both healthy and sick animals by myself.

I learned that it was easier to keep a healthy animal healthy than to nurse it back to health. I learned that most sick animals need constant care rather than emergency veterinary care. I found that stress contributed to almost every illness and sometimes was the only cause. Most importantly, I developed a working knowledge of disease transmission, vaccinations, infectious diseases, etc.

The lessons I learned during those years became the basis for my "culture program," which would eventually begin to save the lives of animals everywhere consistently. Though much of my knowledge came from veterinarians and other health care providers, I learned to trust my instincts and judgement as a rule. I questioned everything and absorbed as much knowledge and experience as I could.

I have learned much and made many mistakes that I now know how to prevent. That is why I feel the need to share my knowledge with others. My instincts, knowledge and experience combined with yours can save more of our precious gifts from God.

The art of healing is a gift. It is also a philosophy and sometimes a heavy, painful burden. It is never about egos for it will always keep you humble; nor is it about money for no mother in the world was ever paid for her role as healer. It is not always learned in school, nor does it respect business hours or worldly influence. It carries with it a responsibility to do our best and then to respect the will of God.

Chapter 1

Why a Yorkshire Terrier?

The bond between humans and dogs is like magic. Sharing your life with a dog stretches far beyond just companionship and the exchange of affection. Interaction takes place on more than simply an intellectual level; a dog possesses the ability to reach into our soul and bring out the best of all that is within. Absolute trust and selfless dedication are given to us. Our dog expresses a sensitivity that humans are hard-pressed to match.

Fortunately, we live in a world that, with the exception of a few countries, generally loves dogs. However, that love has its boundaries. England does not love dogs so much that they will not quarantine them for months before they can enter the country. America does not love dogs so much that it is acceptable to bring your Saint Bernard into a department store with you. Our love, sadly enough, has its limits, despite the fact that so many of us consider our dogs part of our family, almost another person in many cases.

The fact remains that we are bonded spiritually with our dogs, sharing a oneness that defies understanding or explanation and seems to exist between dog and owner from the moment we set eyes on each other. We want to be with them much as we are with our brother, mother or grandfather. Obviously when we are traveling or shopping, running at the beach or having a picnic in the park, we like our four-legged friends to accompany us. So many times we have limitations placed on our togetherness.

One of the best ways I can think of to overcome the limitations imposed by society lies in the world of the Yorkshire Terrier. Why choose a Yorkshire Terrier over all the other breeds out there?

Why A Yorkshire Terrier?

Ask yourself these questions before you make this commitment. What is the dog's purpose in your life and lifestyle? Do you want a companion? How many people are in the home? Are there small children in the home? If you are grandparents, do small grandchildren come to visit? Are the children in the family very active such as boys that want to run and play in the yard with a family dog? Is the Yorkie going to be a companion to an invalid? Is this Yorkie going to be a best friend to a young teenage girl? Is the Yorkie a gift from a boyfriend? Who will it belong to if they break up? If buying a female, is this Yorkie a large expense where there would be a desire to breed her to 'get your money back'? Can the budget handle the necessary expenses that will come with a new pet?

Personality

One of the most wonderful characteristics of a Yorkshire Terrier and one that I noticed immediately is that they look you right in the eye. So many other dogs will look away in the Beta (submissive) demeanor; in other words, they will glance at you and look away so as not to make direct eye contact. A Yorkie not only looks you right in the eye but will hold the eye contact until *they* lose interest.

In canine behavior, eye contact is considered a challenge to the other individual and usually the prelude to a confrontation. The individual that breaks the locked stare first is considered to be the submissive one of the two. In the case of Yorkies, they are not putting out a challenge for battle with you, but instead are involving themselves in each decision. They are totally interested in your opinion and want you to be interested in theirs (for after all that is what they are telling you: "their opinion"). They interact with you in so many ways that the communication is clear and unmistakable.

When they want to say something to you, they will not let you off the hook until they get your attention. If you teach them a game such as "go get the ball," you had better be ready for them to have more stamina than you do. Once they get the idea, there is no such thing as them playing with you anymore, it is you playing with them. They are animated in body, bark, and looks. Many years ago, I was told that a dog that "talks with its paws" is very smart; if that is true then Yorkies are wizards. They actually create new games where *they* figure out the game.

My sweet Tommy would get up on the couch and would "doozle" under the couch cover or sweater that might be on the couch. You could see the movement of his little body under the cover while he went first one way then the other. I'd say "Tommy! Peek a Boo!" and then he'd pop his head out of the cover and give me this incredible look like, "You rang?" That was how he earned his name "Champion Lemire's Peeping Tom."

For those that don't know about "doozling" a Yorkie puts her head down on the top of the skull right behind the eyes (right where their topknot is supposed to be) and rubs back and forth or around in a circle, trying to get their bow or ribbon out. It seems to be a breed characteristic as I have never seen another breed do this. And they all seem to be born with the talent and desire to wreck their pretty little faces the mo-

ment you are not looking or immediately after you have gotten their bow in just right!

Another Yorkie of mine, Cari, would claim my sweater for her trophy. I'd lay it on the couch. She'd go over and make a nest in it. All this would look innocent until I'd go to pick it up and that was when she would growl real low. It was not a menacing, real kind of growl, but a playful, challenging kind that said "the game was on." She is definitely the Alpha girl in our house.

Yorkies love attention and are very entertaining to watch but they are also not so demanding that they become a nuisance. Some dogs you might get to the point where you have to lock them up to get some peace and quiet, but Yorkies are very tuned into the moods and activity cycles of their owners. When you want to take a nap-guess what!! They do too!

Another great thing about a Yorkie is their versatility. This little dog can blend with whatever their situation is. I know people who take their Yorkie on a motorcycle (in their jacket), or on a sailing boat (complete with her scarf to protect from the wind). One of my Yorkies that I placed with a loving couple has been to France twice with them (France is more forgiving about pet entry than England). Once there he goes everywhere with them in Europe.

Size

Yorkies are lightweight, a real advantage for people with back problems (like myself) and people that want a smaller package. Typically, a Yorkie will range in size from three to seven pounds. When I got my first Yorkies it was because I had back problems and could no longer handle raising German Shepherds. They just "beat me up" even when they were playing with me. I couldn't even take them for a walk because they would jerk me around. Yorkies are easy to handle, agile, and jump in my lap so I don't have to bend to pick them up.

This size factor also makes them very portable which is lovely if you want to have a companion that can go places with you. I can't count the number of times I have had one of my Yorkies with me in a restaurant, tucked away quietly in its carrying case under the table while I enjoyed a peaceful meal. A Yorkie can become accustomed to many diverse situations; it only depends on what you do with your Yorkie that determines how easily it adapts to new places and faces. All Yorkies are intelligent enough to learn to travel well, whether this means across the country or just down the street for a leisurely lunch.

Size is also important to people who are looking for a dog that fits into their particular living situation. What if you are in a studio apartment or a small house? You don't have to give up having a pet because a Yorkie is perfect for small spaces. And they are so intelligent, they can be trained to go potty outside or inside on a pee pad.

Easy to exercise

Although a conditioned Yorkie is capable of running 6-9 miles in one stretch, the fact that it is such a small dog can make its exercise demands less than that of a larger dog. The exercise it gets inside the house is usually sufficient, although a trip to the park or the beach and your Yorkie may just have found paradise!

Allergies

Yorkshire Terriers are wonderful dogs for people with allergies as they have hair instead of fur. This reduces the allergic response in many people who cannot tolerate other, fur-bearing breeds. Because of the hair that they grow, they also do not shed as fur-bearing dogs do. That means no dog hair on your clothes or all over your house. They also do not have "doggie" odor like many other breeds. I find this much more pleasant to be around when you hug them and have them in your lap. They don't make your house have that doggie odor either. All this means Yorkies are generally easy to live with.

Good for Your Health

For many people, dogs are not only an important source of love and friendship, but are good for our health. Obviously we can benefit from the regular exercise of walking a dog. However, it is not commonly known that over the last 30 years, increasing scientific evidence shows that dogs can help to keep us fit and well, and even help speed up recovery after a major illness.

A recent 10-month study at Cambridge University found that owning a pet improved the general health of a person in as little as one month. Pet owners were found to suffer fewer ailments, such as headaches, colds and hay fever.

Even more significantly, many people who own pets are better able to survive major health challenges such as heart disease and heart attacks. In fact, according to an American study, pet ownership proved to be one of the best predictors of survival from a heart attack.

The study showed that those patients who owned a pet had a much better chance of surviving for more than a year after a heart attack—a difference which could not be explained by the extra exercise the dog owners enjoyed.

In a recent issue of *Active Living* in Portland, Oregon, an article was written about how some insurance companies are even waking up to the possibility that a pet is beneficial to your health. You may even receive lower premiums by owning a pet and what better pet than a Yorkie?

Travel & Local Trips

The Baby Boomers have fallen in love with the world of toy dogs in the last decade. One reason is that they travel so well. Since many of the young seniors have taken to the road in RVs of various kinds, some of them are on the go constantly. A small, portable, easy-care dog that is intelligent and full of personality makes a perfect traveler.

But no matter what your age, you will find the Yorkshire Terrier an easy companion. With the advent of the Sherpa bag (and with the more expensive Louis Vuitton dog carrier), the Yorkie is a "go anywhere" pet. The Sherpa bag is a perfect hiding place if you are inside a store, and a great retreat if your little friend tires of walking. It also gives protection from cold, rain, snow and wind for that little traveler. In addition, the Sherpa bag is approved for use on most airlines if you aren't driving to your next vacation spot.

Seniors

I think of a Yorkie as a reward, in a way. They are such a treat in life that I think of them as that particularly rich and sinful dessert after dinner. They are what spoils us and appeals to our sweet tooth. This is especially true if we are among the seniors of the world who have eaten of the hearty meals, the meat and potatoes, so to speak. We've had our days of German Shepherds, Labradors, and Spaniels.

As we move into the second half of our lives, we seem to cut down on our portions, instead splurging on delicacies and favorites. We look for quality instead of quantity. We eat for today and put aside the era of making jellies and filling the freezer with vegetables home grown in the garden. Now we are ready to reward ourselves for all the hard work of raising our children and working for thirty or forty years.

I think that as senior citizens give up so much of their turf, large homes, big yards, big cars, big paychecks, 16 oz. steaks, large dogs and endless family and chores, they find themselves downsizing. We don't need to put the pressure on ourselves of handling everything all at once, with health limitations, vision diminishing, budgeting, and families that move away and live their own lives.

Whether it's a puppy or an adult, a wonderful bundle of energy and love like a Yorkie can breathe new life into this smaller world. They are totally dependent on us for their whole world. They respond to our every word with total interest. They don't care about how we look, whether we wear the latest fashions, or are getting gray. They don't judge us by our spending, activity, health, dress or any other superficial thing.

19

They just love us and respect us. They develop a huge vocabulary (speaking on doggie terms) and they listen devotedly for a word that they will recognize and be able to react to. I find myself spelling around them so they don't go nuts when I say a fun word like "bye bye" or "outside." That puts them in a frenzy. They give 100 percent plus and notice everything that goes on around them.

I think seniors take a small amount of comfort in being able to control a small part of their world that they can hold dear. To feel needed and depended upon is like going back in time to having a baby when they needed us for everything. It is completing a full circle. The bonus is that this time they don't cry, or grow up and borrow the car. It is hard to let go of our children sometimes and be left behind as they go their way, and a Yorkie (or two) can make our world bright and fun again.

Plus, that precocious little terrier is fearless and ever so smart. They are dedicated and protective of us on the same level as a Rottweiller and as intelligent as a Poodle. Yorkies take us from considering the personal and mundane to glimpsing a better understanding of the universal. How do they do this? They look straight at us, unafraid of meeting our eyes, and challenge us to get inside *their* minds instead of being stuck in our own. One of the greatest gifts Yorkies give older people is the ability to think about something else other than our own daily problems. This can be lifesaving! It is a fact that people with high blood pressure can lower their blood pressure with the help of a Yorkie. I consider them like health insurance because all that attention and devotion can be just what the doctor ordered.

Yorkies as Service Dogs

If you are a senior and you don't move too well, if you are handicapped and have to walk with a cane, walker or in a wheelchair, a Yorkie is great for you. This little dog is not only bursting for love for you regardless of how you look or what you can do, it is a devoted and loyal companion who will protect you and be sensitive to your individual needs.

For instance, Yorkies are great "service" dogs for seniors with hearing problems. When seniors wear hearing aids during the day, they must take them out at night to sleep. Then they have little ability to hear if the phone rings, the doorbell rings or the smoke alarm goes off. A Yorkie is a great little alarm for these occasions.

Did you know that there are several agencies around the country that can test and certify your Yorkie for work in nursing homes? Along with the certification comes an insurance policy that protects you from liability in the case of accidents. So you see, you and your Yorkie may have lots of love just waiting to give and lots of people waiting to get it.

Yorkies are like chicken soup. No one knows exactly why they make you feel better, they just do. I

In July 1990, I paid a very small price for a skinny little six-week-old Yorkie from a local breeder. This was not a practice I usually engaged in, but I just wanted a gentle, tempered "junk" dog to keep my expensive show Yorkies company. Into

21

my life came Candy.

Candy had a poor start in life, fighting his way back from a severe bacterial infection. At six months, he chewed up a pencil and had to have $800 worth of surgery to dislodge a wood splinter from his intestines. To my vet's amazement, he lived. Not only was he a tough little guy, but it quickly became apparent that he was also the smartest Yorkie I ever owned.

We enrolled in a local obedience class. After an excellent start for both owner and dog, one night while practicing the down-stay command, a boxer leapt across the field of dogs. He lifted Candy in his jaws and shook him like a small chew toy. More vet bills and a terrified little dog.

After that we practiced in the quiet of our own yard for a while. But somehow I knew Candy deserved more.

Candy became a docent in the public school system. We were an animal rescue foster home and he always accepted every foster dog we housed with no animosity. One night Candy went out to potty and returned with a cat that remained and lived with us for two years.

But Candy's greatest joy was the nursing home visitation program. He loved those people and they loved him. His little tail would start to wag the moment he realized where we were. Several hours of holding, kissing and hugging always ensued. He was a master! Four pounds of joy just waiting to be shared.

Today I thank Candy for nurturing me through a painful divorce, nursing me through surgery and giving so thoroughly of himself to me and to others. Candy, you have more heart than I could have ever imagined possible.

(by Kris Dickinson)

Chapter 2

Finding Your Yorkie

Before you step foot out the door or pick up the phone to begin looking for a puppy or dog, make your list of priorities—size, coat type, gender, color, age—and keep referring back to it. I learned a great deal about understanding and evaluating young puppies by comparing them to the parents. If you are not allowed to see the parents, that could be a red flag. After all, why would they have to hide one of the dogs from you? Of course, if someone else owns the sire (dad), you may only get to see the dam (mother).

The florist's son handed his teacher a gift. She shook it overhead and said, "I bet I know what it is—some flowers." "That's right," the boy said, "but how did you know?" "Oh, it was just a wild guess," the teacher replied.

The next pupil was the candy store owner's daughter.

The teacher held her gift overhead, shook it and said, "I bet I can guess what it is—a box of candy." "That's right, but how did you know?" asked the girl. "Oh, just a wild guess," the teacher answered.

The next gift was a large box from the son of the liquor store owner. The teacher started to hold it overhead, but it was leaking. She touched a drop of the leakage to her finger and tasted it. "Is it wine?" she asked. "No," the boy replied. Puzzled, the teacher repeated the process, touching another drop of the leakage to her tongue. "Is it champagne?" she asked. "No," the boy replied. The teacher then said, "I give up. What is it?" The boy replied happily, "It's a puppy!"

SIZE

Sometimes people have a picture of what they think is "the perfect Yorkie" in their minds before they even start searching. Other times, they are open to the first dog that captures their heart. There has been a trendy rage lately to find what I call "tinies" or "Betty Boops." These are Yorkies that will not reach more than two or three pounds by the time they are full-grown.

Breeders are also feeding the trend fires when they charge outrageous, four figure sums for these dogs that are viewed in many cases as no more than novelty items. While everyone thinks they want a pocket pet, the reality of these Yorkies is that they are veterinary nightmares! If you are not prepared to potentially be up all night, willing to be home a majority of the time and ready to deal with a dog that could have the tendency to be hypoglycemic (low blood sugar), a tiny is not for you.

Tinies versus Standard

It seems that for the last ten to twenty years, the smaller the better and the more expensive. Is that the way it should be? That thinking and practice has caused many breeders, both show and backyard as well as puppy mill breeders, to make an effort to breed the tiny little Yorkies that top the scale at 3 to 3.5 pounds as adults. What is the result of this kind of encouraged deviation from what would be considered 'normal' size?

When Yorkies were first being bred in the United States, they were accepted in the show ring up to 12 pounds. At one point, they were shown in two classes: five and under and five to 12 pounds. You could assume that if dogs were allowed to be shown at 12 pounds, they were probably produced from breeding stock that went up to 18 pounds. Eventually, they lowered the show weight standard to one class: "not to exceed 7 pounds." That predisposed the breeders and owners to begin to "breed down" to try to reduce the size of the offspring.

With this reduction in the size of Yorkies came the occasional smaller puppy and they became a novelty. Of course they were darlings; how could they not be? The fact that they are adorable and seem overly animated makes them enchanting. We always seem to be fascinated by the young of any species, like puppies, kittens, bear cubs, fawns and even baby elephants. It seems like the tiny ones of any breed are reminiscent of the babies of the breed.

Because tinies are not normal, but the exception, they have become special, desirable, a novelty, and therefore have become increasingly expensive. I remember when my grandmother was still here, she always had a toy poodle as a companion. These were not the ordinary toy poodle, but the "teacup" poodle. These tiny poodles became very expensive because they are not normal size. Poodles have been bred down in size from the standard poodle with their grace and stature to two other accepted sizes, the miniature and the toy poodle. But the toy poodle is about 9 to 10 pounds (on average) standing 10 inches tall at the withers (shoulder) and this was still too big for the public who wanted the little 6 to 7 inch tall teacups.

So this seemed to separate the show breeders from the pet breeders. A tiny teacup poodle would be useless to a toy poodle breeder since it is too tiny to breed or show. The pet breeders didn't want those 10-inch tall poodles that were too big to attract the big money. Plus they would be competing for the market with the show breeders who were selling their pet quality puppies to the public. Better, they thought, to breed for small size and have no competition in the market from show breeders.

A similar situation exists with the Yorkie breed and many health problems have arisen with this size reduction. Now you would think that as you reduce the size of the offspring by reducing the size of the parents that all would be reduced at the same rate. Not so. As size comes down, especially if it comes down fast, the heart, brain, and bone structure might not come down at the same rate. This brings on conditions like an enlarged heart or hydrocephalus, which I discuss at length in Chapter 10.

As the size of show dogs was expected to come down to 7 lbs. and under, more and more 'teacup' Yorkies were produced. They started selling these little guys for higher prices than the normal sized dog. They were called exotic. The same complications began to befall the Yorkies that were plaguing the Toy Poodle.

I see these little guys being sold for anything from $800 to $2,000 and people think that this is acceptable. These little ones actually might require huge vet bills to handle any problems that come up. My first vet explained that if a crisis came up for a little one, it was like operating on a hummingbird. Anesthesia was risky, hypoglycemia a probability, and even getting a needle in the vein (catheter) could be impossible.

Pocket Rocket's Story

I had a very tiny Yorkie puppy born that I named Pocket Rocket. He was so adorable, but I was afraid to think about placing him in a home. He was about 5 or 6 months old and I kept hoping he would grow more, but I was also afraid that he would grow too much and develop an enlarged heart. I had to keep feeding him every two or three hours, usually baby food mixed with other combinations like Science Diet Puppy. His teeth were way too small to crunch into kibble.

One day a lady came to my home looking for a Yorkie puppy. She saw Pocket Rocket and fell in love. I told her he was not for sale. When she asked why and if I would reconsider, I explained that he was a problem on wheels. He had to be hand fed constantly and could never be left alone for more than two hours. He could go down with hypoglycemia from something as simple as having a shot or teething. These or other kinds of stress eat up their energy.

She said that he would be perfect for her and began to explain why. She told me that her husband was dying of cancer and was on many medications. He was so ill that he rarely slept for more than an hour and was usually up all night in pain, therefore keeping her awake as well. She didn't mind helping him get through his illness, but it was sapping her strength to watch him suffer and know an unhappy ending lay ahead. Each day became a burden for her heart.

She explained that she would be up all night and day, she could never leave her husband alone, and a little guy like Pocket Rocket would be a blessing to her. He could entertain her, keep her company, and give her a diversion from her despair. She didn't mind that he would require so much individual attention.

I sold him to her for $200.00 because I told her he was a day-today proposition. I explained that I could not 'guarantee' his health or that he would live a normal life. I gave her special instructions about his schedule and diet. She was so thrilled that I could see the grey hollow expression on her face fading away as she picked him up and adopted him in her heart. Barely looking at me, she floated out the door with her darling cradled in her hands. She cooed at him and laughed at his expression while he tried to lick her face.

I could no more charge her a huge price on this little guy than I could fly. Who knows what kind of vet bills lay ahead for her? I could only hope that whatever time they had together lightened her heart and life, as well as his.

I know that this is a general rule of thumb, but one guideline to determine the weight that a puppy will achieve when full grown is this formula: an eight week old puppy will triple its weight and possibly add an extra pound. A 12-week old puppy will double its weight and possibly add a pound besides.

If weight as an adult is important to you, go and purchase a gourmet scale before you go looking for a puppy. Be prepared. If you weigh the puppies, do this on the floor so there are no mishaps if a puppy jumps away and gets away from you. In the case of someone who travels a lot by common carrier they might need a pet that is 5 pounds or less because of the ability to carry the animal in a carrier through airports. A person in a wheel chair might need one that is seven to eight pounds that would have the ability to jump up in their lap unassisted.

Adult or Puppy?

My Yorkies are all raised as house dogs so that even after they move past their breeding years, they are still very adaptable to life as a wonderful pet to someone. They make incredible companion dogs. Many breeders are looking for wonderful "retirement homes" for their mature bitches that are past breeding age. Some bitches are retired at age five and others at seven. This may depend on the overall health of each girl and how many litters she has had.

I've never had an unhappy person when they've taken an adult instead of a puppy. People have even called and requested a retiring adult after they saw another one that I placed.

The Puppy For You

In many cases, the breeder you are working with may try to pick the Yorkie puppy for you after discussing with you what you are looking for. A concerned breeder will take into consideration the kind of personality, home, and other aspects of your life. It is in the interest of the breeder to make sure that you get the puppy that best suits you and best for the Yorkie as well.

However, should you have the opportunity to pick your own puppy, avoid picking from litters where even one puppy seems ill. You are looking for healthy, outgoing and active puppies with no evidence of discharge from their noses, eyes or ears. If they are a little cautious when you first approach but then are interested in playing and smelling you, chalk that up to natural fear of new things. Resist your temptation to pick the "runt" of the litter or a puppy that cowers in the corner. Conversely, the Yorkie puppy that rushes to greet you,

29

knocking over anything and anyone in its way may be tough to discipline. Keep in mind what you are looking for and, most importantly, what you will have in the long run.

Although tempting, not everyone should automatically pick the tiniest female as the perfect puppy. Many times, females become "daddy's little girl" so for the man of the house, females are great. Many a woman has purchased a female and ended up watching her bond to "Daddy" instead. Males gravitate to women, as a rule, and if he is neutered, he will be easier to housebreak, so there's no reason to skip over the males in the selection process.

Other Pets

Another factor in having a Yorkie in your home is whether you already have other pets. Some people have a cat, bird, other older dog and so forth. Yorkies usually get along very well with cats, especially if they grow up with them. I would definitely evaluate the personality of the cat as well. There are many cats that are "predators" and they might consider the Yorkie a great challenge (or lunch). We had outdoor cats that killed squirrels, chipmunks, mice, rats, and anything else they could catch. They would bring their latest trophy to the back door (or pieces of the prey) as if to show off their prowess (or maybe share their dinner).

Nevertheless, cats have a great advantage over dogs because of their claws. Cats are much better suited to do battle and a cat can kill a dog much bigger than itself. Cats usually play by using their claws and can injure a dog without even intending to. I know of one Yorkie that got a terrible cut on the eyeball and it was a problem for the dog's entire life. Cats have the ability to climb or jump up on furniture or cabinets to escape the Yorkie and are very agile, but the Yorkie, while agile, is much more earthbound.

The same consideration might be necessary if you have an adult Yorkie and you are planning to get a kitten. Remember that Yorkies are "ratters" by nature (meaning that they were originally bred to kill rats much bigger than themselves) and have a predator nature as well. The adjustment to new members of the family should be monitored very closely in the beginning until a rapport is established.

We had one of our champion bitches that we are positive was responsible for the disappearance of my daughter's parakeet. The bird was loose in the house when they left to go shopping. When they returned home there was no bird. Jackie greeted them at the door with a totally innocent look on her face, but one feather was still stuck to her nose. She didn't leave any trace of that bird, other than the one feather. "What bird? I didn't see any bird! Did you see a bird?? I didn't see a bird!" When I had an aviary, my Yorkies would sit for hours and watch the birds flitting from one branch to the other. I knew what was in their mind.

Children

Again, if children are in the home, and they are rambunctious, mean spirited, rowdy or show bad judgment, then I strongly suggest a larger dog. I consider Yorkshire Terriers to be more of an adult pet as they are very fragile in terms of family activities. With children, you have to consider what kind of friends they have and what their lifestyle is. Boys that play touch football every weekend are probably not going to slow down for a Yorkie and might be more at home with a Golden or Labrador.

What kind of nature and temperament do your children have? I once let a small male Yorkie go into a home with three small girls 4 years to 8 years after meeting them and their mother. These girls were quiet, gentle, well mannered, and very much the "Holly Hobby" types. In the case of a home with active children, I advise you seek a Yorkie in the range of 10 pounds or larger or perhaps consider a larger and sturdier breed. This family needs a more durable, active, agile pet who can easily become "the family dog."

My general rule of thumb has been that Yorkshire Terriers are "adult toys" for the most part and the smaller ones especially are not really designed for a family with children. Many Yorkies do not respond well to small children. They might bark and even try to nip at them. They seem to sense that there might be a danger with the quick movements and loud noises that accompany small children. Many small children seem to want to tease these small little creatures because they respond by jumping about and barking. This can create a "knee jerk reaction" that will continue throughout the life of the Yorkie. My advice is to avoid allowing this behavior to start and if children cannot respect the dog, then the dog should not be there in the first place.

One Yorkie or Two?

Once you make a decision to get a Yorkshire Terrier, the next question seems to come naturally. Should you get a second Yorkie? There's no simple answer. Remember we talked about Yorkshire Terriers being "more terrier than toy"? This is a definite factor when deciding whether to add a second Yorkie to the family.

If you have an adult dog that has been in the family for

a while and is the established "patriarch" or "matriarch"' you need to be very careful about bringing another dog into the picture. I think it is very therapeutic for a "senior" dog to have a youngster around to keep the games going and perk up their lives.

Just remember the number one law of canines: there is always a pecking order. The "alpha dog" and "alpha bitch" are going to be the bosses no matter what. Most of the time the alpha dog will be the one that has been there the longest. Occasionally, a new dog will come into the family and challenge the older dog for the alpha position. That can lead to trouble depending on how aggressive each will be. Size can make a huge difference, too.

Opposites Fit Fine

When you are planning to add another Yorkie to your fold, my advice would be to go for opposites. Never bring in an adult male when you already have an adult male. If you bring in another male, you may see serious challenges for dominance. One or more could be hurt or killed. Never bring in an adult female when you already have an adult female. If you have a female and plan to add another female, this must be done very carefully. Don't think for a minute that just because they are "girls" that they are not able and willing to challenge or even in some cases kill another female that challenges what they see as their territory. If you have a female, you can be pretty safe getting a male and vice versa. If you do bring in a Yorkie of the same sex as the one you already have, it is best that it be a puppy so it will not challenge the alpha dog.

When you bring in a new Yorkie, watch to see how they get along with your other dog(s). Do not leave them alone, even after you have had them for a while; have a cage or exercise pen to separate the new arrival from the others. Also avoid feeding them together as food becomes something to fight over with a newcomer. Make sure fights don't start over toys and give the other dog(s) as much attention as the new arrival.

One time I had two males get into a fight while I went into town. I always separated them by putting one in a playpen. But Thadius could climb out of it and so usually I put Brutus in the playpen. On this occasion, I was in a hurry and forgot. I put Thadius in the playpen and he climbed out. Brutus was the alpha dog and was waiting for Thadius as he would wait for a burgular to come into his territory.

I had just gotten to town (12 miles away) when I had this horrible feeling in my stomach. I *knew* that Thadius was in danger. I drove back as fast as possible and as I drove in the driveway, I looked at the picture window where Brutus usually kept a watch for my return. He wasn't there. I ran into the house and found Thadius pinned down in a corner by Brutus with many bites in his hind legs. Thadius was smaller and inexperienced. If I hadn't returned when I did, Brutus would have killed him.

In another situation, a friend of mine had an alpha bitch and didn't think she would ever harm another dog. She had a tiny three pound female Yorkie that was just a pet. Her older alpha girl didn't like the tiny female, but so far had only growled at her. One day, everyone left and the dogs were alone together in the house. When the lady returned, she found the smaller female dead. A month or so later, the alpha female attacked another female and mutilated her so badly that she had to be put to sleep. When the third attack came against a show dog, the only thing that saved the other dog's life was that the owner returned and stopped a total slaughter.

These are not *bad* dogs. The simple fact is, dogs are dogs no matter how small a package they come in. So you as the loving owner have to know your boundaries and limitations with more than one Yorkie.

Each Yorkie is different and that goes for personalities as well. They are like people; they will like some dogs and they will not tolerate others. Once two dogs have squared off and challenged each other, it is hopeless to ever expect them to get along. They do not ever forgive and forget. If you have two males or two females that challenge each other, you are courting danger to try to keep them in the same house from that moment on. One will lay in wait for a chance to go after the other again. Even if you have fences and cages to separate the two conflicting dogs, they will get sneaky and hide, waiting to pounce when no one suspects anything. They actually become hunters at that point. They never get over it. So if this happens, you should make other plans for one of them to go to a new home.

If you plan to add a female to a home where another female is already established as the matriarch, you have a better chance to bring in a younger female. If they still have that puppy smell (three to eight months) the older female may try to "mother" the new arrival and accept her. They may not ever try to challenge each other because the younger female would automatically accept the older one as the alpha bitch. In that way, the pecking order is already established.

Yorkie Love

It is such a rewarding thing when you see a Yorkie that has been alone react to a new Yorkie and actually establish a special bond of their own. They become like sisters and once the initial adjustment period is over, they usually are bonded forever. They sleep together, play together, tease each other, and compete with each other for your love and attention. This is usually all in good spirit (and if it is not, you know what you have to do).

WHERE TO BUY A YORKIE

Today there are many sources of Yorkshire Terriers as they have become one of the most popular companion dogs of the toy size. You may call the American Kennel Club (AKC) to ask for references of breeders in your area. This is not necessarily an endorsement of the quality of the breeder or the Yorkie. Another source is the local newspaper, while another is a pet store (not recommended). One of my favorite choices is to contact the local dog club (you can ask vets and pet store for referrals to find them) and ask them for references to local breeders. They might also lead you to a local rescue organization. Let's look at what each of these choices has to offer.

AKC Breeder Referral

You can find the number of the AKC either online or in your city's telephone book. When you call the AKC, they will give you names and phone numbers of several people close to you. These might be show breeders or "backyard breeders." They will show no favoritism nor give any reference as to the quality of dogs or breeders. Only names and numbers will be given. That might be a good start. Remember you need to shop around and review all your options.

AKC Dog Clubs

Contacting the local dog club is one of my favorite choices and something that I advise many people to do. Not only are these affiliated with the AKC, which is a stamp of approval that sets them apart from many others, these dog clubs also represent a network of local breeders who generally have an idea of who breeds and when there will be puppies. In addition, the people in the clubs usually know the good breeders and you might get a little hint of what breeders to avoid. They may only give you positive leads and just not give you the names of dubious breeders. It is also a good place to ask questions like, how many dogs are allowed in your city or county, do they need to be licensed, can they recommend a veterinarian, and more.

Dog Shows

Any of the popular dog magazines, including *Dog World, Dog Fancy, AKC Gazette* or *Yorkshire Terrier Magazine* will have listings of national dog shows for each breed. You will likely find one in your area and this is a good place to meet Yorkie breeders. Check your library for issues of these magazines.

The Internet

Again, this is a place to hook up with other Yorkie owners and possibly breeders. This is also a good place for all kinds of information about Yorkies. On America Online, there is a Yorkshire Terrier message board (people post questions and comments about Yorkies). It is not only a nice community to be a part of, but it's also a good place to start in your search for your own Yorkie. Try keyword: dog on AOL and go from there. Keep your eyes open: bad breeders use all means to draw buyers in, too.

Newspaper Ads

Many years ago I watched the newspaper to go check out breeders. I wanted to learn as much as possible about how puppies develop. This is only a good idea if you can be clinical about your choice and not fall in love with the first puppy you get your hands on.

Personal Referrals

I think my most reliable source is the personal referral. If you know someone who has a Yorkie, ask if they would give you any leads as to the breeder they bought from. Word of mouth is the best advertising and I really believe this is true when it come to buying a Yorkie. Sometimes it will not be a good reference and that is good information to know as well.

RESCUE

There are Yorkie "rescue" organizations in most states that work very hard to care for these poor animals when they can be rescued from either puppy mills or are abandoned at animal shelters. How can a Yorkie end up in an animal shelter? Many reasons. None of them justify this outcome. Some people do not have the money to properly care for a dog, or perhaps they are gone all the time and the dog is a nuisance to them. Perhaps the responsibility is more than they bargained for. Maybe it was a gift from someone and they never wanted it in the first place. Perhaps the landlord has threatened to evict them if they don't get rid of the dog. All of these excuses are used to explain or justify how or why these special little creatures are abandoned and abused. Some are found wandering down a road lost and helpless.

These situations might never have happened if the people who thought they wanted a Yorkie had done their own research and found out all the responsibilities that came with getting this little creature. It is not something to enter into lightly. If you decide that you have the ability and love to give a rescue Yorkie a home, that is a wonderful thing to do.

But make sure it is right for you. It takes immeasurable love, patience and compassion to open your home to a rescue Yorkie. Many have never been housebroken (they have lived in chicken coops or wire cages), are terrified of people, and have a variety of health problems. You might not even know the age of this sweet little victim. But the rewards can be overwhelming as you take this refugee and open their world to love and caring. Do not think that because they are "free" (sometimes there is a minimum donation requested) that they will not be expensive. You may have large vet bills from the abuse and neglect that these babies have suffered.

Rescue homes are like halfway houses that take dogs in when they are found and give them the best possible help and love while a permanent home is being sought. If you have a big heart and want to find a rescue Yorkie, you can contact any one of the rescues that I list in the Resources section at the back of this book.

PLACES TO AVOID

Pet Stores & Puppy Mills: A Circle of Sadness

I strongly advise that you avoid buying or even looking at the pet stores for dogs or puppies. Many people cannot resist the pathetic look of puppies in the pet store and that is just what pet stores depend on. Many people regret the decisions made in haste at pet stores. My own daughter made the mistake of doing business with a pet store. Her own little Chihuahua that she had for about three years had gotten out of the front door when company was leaving and had been run over. She lost the pet she loved for years at a very vulnerable time in her life. She knew better than to go to a pet store (she had heard it from me for years) but she was pregnant, emotional, and I was in Canada so she couldn't call me for help.

She bought a little Chihuahua puppy at a local pet store and it was a nightmare. Within four days, the puppy came down with Parvo (incubation time is 5 to 6 days) and after huge vet bills trying to save the puppy, it died anyway. The pet store would not refund her money or give her another puppy.

She was afraid to get another puppy from them anyway because it would have been exposed to the same Parvo as the first one was. Now she was out the puppy, the money, and owed the vet bills not to speak of the heartache of losing that little puppy.

So many times these spontaneous decisions lead to tragedy and regret.

Here's How it Works

Pet stores usually get their puppies from "brokers or puppy mills. Brokers are agents who are in contact with many hundreds of puppy mills. They take the orders and send the puppies out to the pet stores. They might have as many as four hundred puppies in their possession at a time. These puppies are separated from their mothers at six weeks old (if they are lucky) and shipped by air in "litter lots" to pet stores. They are considered a "crop" with these people. The puppies are not socialized and there is certainly no consideration given to staying true to the breed or to temperament.

When the puppies arrive at the pet store, minus any vaccinations of course (no one's going to spend the money on that!), they are exposed to all the viruses and bacterial infections that have come in from every other puppy mill which supplies that store. Now, adult animals with mature immune systems might have a chance to fight all this, but puppies don't have much of a chance at all. Then there are the potential buyers that come in and handle these puppies and if they are carrying parvo, distemper, kennel cough, or corona on their clothes (perhaps from being at another pet store), they will expose those puppies to these illnesses. If that isn't enough, the puppies usually have fleas or worms from their mothers and if they are not treated early, these worm infestations can kill a puppy too.

The average cost to the pet store for these puppy mill puppies is about $50.00 each and then they charge many hundreds of dollars to the public. Even more devastating is that most pet stores have a back room or closet where the sick puppies are kept. Is it likely that they would spend $300.00 in vet bills to save a puppy that cost them $50.00? No way! They would rather just wait for them to die or maybe help them to die. These sick puppies are just part of the business as far as they are concerned.

You can not imagine in your worst nightmares what conditions exist where these poor puppies come from. For instance, the Yorkie lovers on some Internet lists that I am on are currently working to save over 300 dogs and about 50 horses that were discovered at a mill in Tennessee. These mills exist in almost every state. There the dogs have no veterinary care at all, are infected with worms, fleas, skin sores and infections, are never bathed, have ear infections, blindness, mats that smell and must be cut off and worse.

These people do not make their decisions about breeding based on bettering the breeds, but instead on which breeding female produces the most puppies, and her life is totally dependent upon her ability to continue to produce. Bitches in trouble during whelp are not helped, and in this puppy mill they had a field of bones from the animals that died, both horses and dogs.

Since dogs and cats are not part of our "food chain," the government has not intervened with health regulations and inspections of puppy mills and brokers. Maybe they should think in terms of the potential spread of disease between humans and animals and change their view of where their responsibility lies.

What You Can Do

Every time a puppy is bought from a pet store, the buyer participates in sentencing the parents of that puppy to continue to live in agony and pain. The buyer becomes part of the problem and supports it with their money. The best way to put puppy mills out of business is to let their customers (pet stores) know that we don't condone their methods of obtaining and selling animals! Out of sheer compassion, I pray that you will help stop this shame that is big business in our country. Don't be lured by prices that seem lower than breeder prices or by those sad faces! You will only participate in sustaining this vicious circle and bring even more sad faces there.

WAIT FOR THE MAGIC

Patience is the Key

With any of these options, please do not make the mistake of buying the first puppy or dog that you come across. This has led to many heartaches. If a breeder truly cares about their puppies finding the right homes, they will not mind if you check around and go see other puppies. The "magical connection" needs to be there before a final decision is made.

The message here is that you must plan and be willing to do your homework. It means looking at several litters, puppies and adults, checking out many breeders and having lots of patience. We would all love to have that "perfect gift" for our daughter's birthday and oftentimes if the dog is for ourselves, it is admittedly hard to be patient. If you do not give yourself the time to do all of this, you could have huge regrets if your puppy doesn't turn out the way you want and that means healthy and well-adjusted.

Try to think of this as a decision that is more important than buying a new car. With a new car you can fix it if it breaks, have warranties included, sell it or trade it in if you don't like it in a year or two. A new Yorkie in your life is a decision you will have to be happy with for many, many years. It reminds me of "for better or worse, in sickness and in health, till death do us part." That is the kind of commitment you are undertaking. Take your time!!!

FINDING A BREEDER

Reputable vs. Backyard Breeders

A puppy is only as good as its breeder. You may hear a lot of controversy concerning who is a "reputable" breeder and who is a backyard breeder. Show breeders are usually considered to be the reputable breeders but I have not necessarily found it to be so. I don't mean to say that there are not reputable show breeders out there who are wonderful people and a great asset to the breed, but do not assume that someone is a reputable breeder just because they show dogs.

I know of many show (i.e. reputable) breeders that I would never sell a dog to—never mind buy a dog from. I also know of many show breeders that I admire and would love to know more about. Probably the hardest decision is who is reputable and who is not. Most reputable breeders breed Yorkies because they are head over heels in love with the breed. They want nothing but the best for the dogs as individuals and as a whole breed. That is why you may instinctively feel better about dealing with a breeder who is open about answering and asking questions when you come to visit.

By the same token, if I were buying a pet, I would give strong thought to checking out the local backyard breeders as well as the show breeders. This means that you must be very careful about what you are seeing. Check out the parents, ask for references, see where the puppies are raised, and what the home is like. Are the dogs kept in a clean, well-lighted area? Are the puppies socialized with the other dogs? What is the behavior of the dogs like? Do they run happily around or do they cower in corners? What about the bitch and/or sire of the puppy you are interested in? Are they clean and friendly? How does this person interact with the dogs?

You would want to see all that you could about the breeder, know what their experience is, be aware of what their guarantee is like (read their contract), talk to their vet, and check the pedigrees and paperwork of their dogs. I know it seems like there are so many things that you need to do in order to make this decision, but it is one of the most important things you can do, both for yourself and your dog.

Don't fall for being shown a show picture on the mantel. I have had at least two show pictures copied from me and used by unscrupulous breeders to sell puppies both on the Internet and real life.

Some cautions about these so-called backyard breeders. Motives for even having the dogs vary. If they are not out to make a profit, then they may just be careless or misguided people. Maybe they bred their bitch to have a litter and show the kids "the miracle of birth." Or maybe they forgot to spay their Yorkie bitch and had a "surprise" litter. Or they are just selfish and wanted a replica of the mom.

At any rate, do you really think these people will stand behind their litter? Remember, even though you may pay less for your Yorkie at a pet store or from a backyard breeder, in the long run, you can bet you will pay more at the vet. And your emotional bills will be high as well, should you have to euthanize a Yorkie because of its health. Your awareness of these things will influence whether you choose to buy from a certain breeder or to keep looking.

Above all, no matter what direction you go in search of your new friend, know the questions to ask about size, health, structure, temperament, etc. Also be sure to talk to at least one or two other people who have bought dogs from the breeder you are in contact with.

What a Breeder Should Do for You

Wherever you decide to purchase your Yorkie, you need to know what guarantee is provided by the breeder. What does separate unethical breeders and good breeders is that good breeders will replace a puppy with an equal or better puppy if a problem arises that threatens your puppy's life or long term health. A responsible breeder will also ask you to return the puppy to her or him if things don't work out—for whatever reason—rather than have you try to re-sell it.

If a puppy is ill or faces long-term problems, a good

45

breeder will give you the option of keeping the problem puppy at no charge and replace it with a good puppy. This would be valuable only if you wanted to keep it of course.

Recently, a story came to me of a lady who had purchased a small Yorkie; he was 17 weeks old and weighed one and a half pounds. The breeder had him practically living on Nutri Cal and he went into a coma less than a week after the new owner got him home. The report from the vet was that the little guy had a liver shunt, which made sense given the fact that he hadn't grown normally. The breeder offered to take back the puppy and give the lady her money back.

To me, this is too little, too late. As a responsible breeder, I would have expected her not to sell the puppy in the first place! A dog with this kind of health problem will be expensive and possibly heartbreaking should surgery not help him live a normal life. The breeder *knew* that the puppy was not healthy; that's why the Nutri-cal was used so often. Why was this breeder not honest enough to tell this lady, 'this dog's future is uncertain and I don't want to sell it to you unless you're ready for that kind of responsibility'? Or I don't want to sell you the dog at all!

Anyway, this is just one example of a breeder that has put the buyer in a position of not only paying for a sick dog, but also shouldering the responsibility of potentially having to put a dog down for health reasons. This is not the kind of breeder that you want to buy a Yorkie from. Your breeder should be an ally, not an enemy.

Interviewing the Interviewer

Don't be surprised if you get asked a few questions as well. The reputable breeder will have the best interest of the dog and the breed in mind. It would not be uncommon to be asked such questions as: 1) Are you familiar with any health problems that might be prevalent in Yorkies? If not, prepare to be educated. 2) Do you have a fenced yard? Yorkies are adept at jumping, digging and generally wriggling their way out of places, so make sure your yard is adequate. 3) Will your Yorkie be a house dog? I would say most Yorkie breeders will not sell to someone who does not keep a Yorkie inside the house. 4) Are you aware of how big the dog will be as an adult? Hopefully, you have researched the breed at least enough to know that much. 5) Are you familiar with the temperament of Yorkies? Some people want a submissive, quiet dog; others want an active one and Yorkies can fit either one if you are clear with the breeder what you are looking for. 6) Does everyone in your home want a Yorkie (or a dog at all)? If not, either someone in the family or the dog is not going to have a happy life! All household members need to agree that they want and welcome a new Yorkie or it should not happen.

Cherry's Story

I had an experience that will haunt me forever. I had a lovely little female that was about 6 months old. She was a real charmer and reminded me of a little butterfly. She would fly through the air when she went outside so utterly joyous at the grass, insects, toys, other dogs, breezes, and sunshine. She flittered from one thing to the next, just loving her life in her own little world.

I'd decided that she was going to be too small to breed by that time and lo and behold a lady contacted me wanting a small female as a companion (pet). I arranged to show little Cherry to her. It seemed love at first sight. This puppy was in love with the world and the new owner seemed delighted with her whole demeanor.

Six weeks went by and all seemed well. Then I got the call. I listened with tears in my eyes as this lady told me the horrible truth of what had happened to Cherry. Apparently, her husband did not want a dog and was resentful of

Cherry. The lady had gone to work and had gotten a call from her husband that she needed to come home. Cherry was not acting right. When she got home, Cherry was paralyzed from the middle of her body back. She rushed her to the vet and upon examining her, he found many bruises as well as broken back and broken ribs. This little 3-pound angel had been slammed in the sliding glass door. The vet had to put her to sleep to end her misery and stop her pain.

We were all so shocked and astounded as well as grief stricken. Cherry was such a sweetheart!!! How could anyone be so cruel??? The husband was not going to accept this little creature into his life, so he killed her. I told the woman that she should consider getting rid of such a man since she could be next. I was in shock at such cruelty.

But this brings up a point that all members of a family have an effect (both good and bad) on the life of these tiny little creatures when they enter a new home. For some it is joy and happiness, but there are times like for Cherry where there is no love at all, only meanness, jealousy, and terror. In other cases, there is neglect and pain.

I've heard so many horror stories about dogs that are abandoned, tortured, cold, hungry, hurting, lonely, lost and almost dead. That is why breeders should spend more time evaluating the home that our dogs will go into and make sure that the door is left open for the dog to be returned if it doesn't work out well. We should be willing to take a dog back and resettle it for the buyers at any point. And this is why, if you are a novice to the Yorkie world, you should be dealing with a breeder who will take the dog back if necessary.

Breeder Contracts & Papers

A contract protects both the breeder and the buyer. Much of what is in a contract has to do with health guarantees, temperament and responsibilities of the breeder. Many contracts also include a spay/neuter clause. You should know that there is most likely nothing wrong with a dog that has this in their contract. When a Yorkie is sold as a pet, it may have what is called a "fault" (overbite, drop ears, etc.) and the breeder does not want it to continue to be bred into the Yorkie line.

In my contract, I am clear in defining the quality of the Yorkie. There are three categories in my opinion: "show quality," "breeding quality" and "companion or pet quality." Some people ask me what the difference is. Many times the difference is the price and the guarantee. That means that sometimes a show quality puppy is sent to a pet home because I felt the home would be best for the dog.

If a person is buying for show quality, they need a very good guarantee concerning the health, both current and future, on the animal. They also need a guarantee that the physical qualities of the animal will be within the parameters and requirements to allow it to be showable and finishable. These contracts can be very complex as many breeders also want guarantees from the buyers that they will properly maintain, show, and finish this animal. Many a show dog was ruined by improper coat care and training, so it could never become a champion. On the other hand, many people buy show quality dogs and the animals have improper "confirmation" (the AKC-approved aspects of a dog) for showing and by the time the owners know it, they love the pet and can't part with it.

My advice for people wanting a show puppy is that they should consider buying a bitch with breeding quality, do the best breeding possible and breed their own litter to have the pick for themselves to show. Most breeders will not part with their best puppies as they want to show them themselves so will only sell second or even third pick to others. Some breeders sell puppies that aren't even born yet based strictly on the pedigree of the parents. Don't get caught in that marketing ploy.

You need to see the registration papers of the parent or parents that the breeder owns. It is important that you ask the right questions about the registration of this puppy or adult. Since AKC now allows pets to be registered as non-breeders, it is not necessarily a reason for breeders to withhold papers until spaying or neutering is complete.

Breed Quality Puppies

When a puppy is sold as breeding quality, in my opinion, it should be show quality or very close to it with possibly having a slight imperfection. That might mean that they are slightly oversized, might go a little light in color, or something aesthetic like that. Remember it is the guarantee that is the determining factor. If the animal can be replaced later on by another great puppy from a future litter, then show or breed quality can be backed up by a replacement puppy.

But when a breeder has very few litters, they might not be able to replace a dog with another one. Then they would have to be ready and willing to refund the purchase price if an animal were to end up not being show or breed quality. Do not think that a show quality puppy is 'perfect' because there aren't any perfect dogs. It is the kind of fault and how it affects the animal that you need to be aware of. They are all different.

Pet Quality Puppies

If the puppy is guaranteed as pet quality, that means that they are not represented to be show or breeding quality and the registration paper of these animals should reflect a non-breeding status. The buyer should be totally aware of this. It is also important that the buyer be aware of what makes this puppy pet quality. Are they going to go oversize (seven pounds is maximum weight for show quality according to the AKC standard)? Do they have light pigment? Is their coat woolly or too light? Are they too terrier, too small, ears too big, bad bite, or what? Disclosure of what the fault is could be very important especially if health issues are involved.

A reputable breeder will be honest and disclose what the nature of the problem or fault (as we call it) is. If it is just aesthetic (meaning color, coat, or such), then there is not a problem as long as you are informed and agree that this will not bother you. But if it is a fault that could affect health, then that needs to be taken into consideration. You would want to consult with a veterinarian about any possible health problems that you suspect or that the breeder might disclose.

If the puppy has something like a slight overbite or underbite, these things, if not extreme, most likely will not have any adverse effect on the life or health of the pet. But if the animal has slipping stifles (patellas) that needs to be looked at carefully. Many toy dogs have slipping stifles (knee caps) and are not affected by it through life. Others might be affected to the point that they need to have surgery done to correct the problem. This is expensive and requires a good deal of recuperation so consulting a veterinarian before jumping into this problem is advisable.

The biggest factor in this decision would be if the dog favors one leg or carries its leg in an unusual way. This would put extra pressure on the good leg and might cause a serious injury to the good leg. Remember that Yorkies are very active and will compensate rather than give in to a disability. Talk to your vet about the possible outcomes related to slipping patellas.

Overall, it's important to keep your eyes open about the different aspects of quality when looking for your Yorkie.

Vet Check

It is a good idea to have the Yorkie checked by your vet while still new enough to be returned if the heart or lungs don't check out. A 24-hour guarantee is ridiculous to say the least. I would always take a puppy back if the buyer was not satisfied, if the buyer's circumstances changed or if the vet found a problem. I wouldn't want one of my dogs to be in a home where they were not loved and appreciated. I especially do lots of follow up on placing adults (retired from breeding or showing) because it can be a little harder for an adult to bond with a new owner. I usually have the new owner take the dog home for a few days or a weekend (while I hold their check) to make sure that they feel comfortable with their decision. Since Yorkies have the ability to adapt easily and can love many people, they rarely come back to me because of problems with settling in to the new home.

When to Bring the Puppy Home

A puppy is very vulnerable to contracting Parvo between 8 and 14 weeks. Exposure to Parvo can happen in ways you wouldn't even think of. It's as easy as a friend who had contact with a sick dog coming to visit and playing with your dog. Because of this reason, primarily, I recommend that a breeder keep a puppy until 16 weeks or more. When I hear of puppies being sent to a new home at 7 and 8 weeks, I am appalled. Most new owners are not knowledgeable enough to take care of a puppy that young.

A 7-week old Yorkie is just cutting its teeth, being weaned from its mother, having its first vaccinations, adjusting to new food and the world. To spring upon them a completely new environment and new people is too much, in my opinion. It can leave the dog bewildered and fearful, and you want a Yorkie that is confident and adapts well to new situations.

Although you obviously need to visit the vet, even this trip is risky until the age of 20 weeks. Some precautions you can take are to keep the puppy inside your pet cab/pet carrier and isolate yourself to every extent possible from other animals in the office. Veterinarians obviously see many animals during the day, so you may want to schedule an early morning appointment when it's not as likely to be crowded. I have even gone so far as to wipe the examining table down with alcohol or, with a smile and a brief explanation, ask the assistant to clean it. They usually don't mind because they understand you are only trying to protect your fragile new creature. I have also brought a blanket or towel from home to cover the exam table with (I'll wash these with Odor Handler when I get home from the vet).

WHEN THE DOLLAR SIGNS FLY

I'm always baffled by what people pay for their Yorkie. In fact many people won't even tell you what they pay because it's usually too much for what they get. It is not uncommon for women to lie about what they pay for their Yorkie. They sneak the money to you and don't want you to say anything in front of the "hubby." I think that the price for puppies or dogs should reflect the quality, size, sex, age and disposition of each pet. If a litter is priced all the same, I would have to wonder about the breeder's knowledge of the breed and/or their own puppies. I believe in "truth in selling" and if I sell a puppy, I want the buyer to know why it is priced the way it is.

For instance, a larger male puppy will usually be priced for less than a female puppy, while a retired adult female might be priced for less than a larger male puppy. Females are customarily priced higher because they are more in demand and less available, not because they are better pets.

As I said earlier, I have heard from people who purchased a so-called tiny Yorkie for upwards of $800 to $2,000. Whew! All I can say is that it can vary from location to location. For instance, in Los Angeles, if you want a Yorkie that will be no more than a pound or two as an adult, brace yourself. You will pay at least $1,500. On the other hand, if you are in Portland, Oregon and you just want a pet sized Yorkie, say, four to eight pounds, and a female, the average price seems to hover around $400 to $600. At this time, I have seen the prices range from $275 to $3,000.

CO-OWNERSHIP?

You may encounter a breeder who sees you fall in love with one of his or her show dogs and offers to become co-owners with you. That means you pay to share that dog, but it is not always with you. It has to spend a great deal of its time being bathed and groomed, trained for showing, traveling, etc. While this situation is more apt to occur between professionals in the show field, it can also happen to novices to the Yorkie breed.

One time a lady I knew went to a breeder's house and saw many dogs running all over the place. One dog in particular caught her eye. A spry little baby boy, he hopped from place to place, filled with energy and incredibly cute. She immediately was drawn to him and offered several times to buy him from the breeder, at even a higher price than she was asking for the other dogs. She fell in love with that puppy!

The breeder did not want to let him go, so instead she said that she and the lady could co-own the dog. When the lady asked what that meant, the breeder basically explained that for the privilege of giving her money, the lady had to surrender the dog to daily grooming sessions and show handlers at least half the time. Obviously, this is not an ideal situation for someone who wants a pet. So be cautious and watch out for your heart when you start looking for a companion.

Digging in the Dirt

If the breed leaders, primary breeders, and respected show breeders with great or good bloodlines are going to hide behind the fact that "puppy mill breeders" are not governed or regulated by the government in order to justify having a blind eye to doing the same thing that puppy mill breeders are doing—breeding genetically inferior or defective dogs regardless of the pain, despair, death and deception that is the result—why do they consider themselves any different than the puppy mills? Perhaps the only difference is the price they charge.

We cannot believe-and go on living with ourselves-that "bad breeders" should not be held accountable. However, as leaders in the Yorkie breeding world, we are responsible for cleaning up our own yards first. We can help ourselves and benefit the breed by patrolling our own waters...by breeding sound dogs and by not breeding when we find a genetic fault. In the end, awareness and information will save everyone involved a great deal of heartache.

Chapter 3

Preparing for Your New Yorkie

You have heard the saying, "a stitch in time saves nine." The same thing applies for the pre-Yorkie household. Before the grand arrival of your little darling, be it a puppy or rescue dog, certain things need to be in place. You need to look at your house through the eyes of your new "four on the floor." Get down on your hands and knees if you have to and just imagine what she could get into! I'll spend this chapter overhauling your house and yard in preparation for the new baby.

I also advise that you start looking for a veterinarian well before your Yorkie comes home. That way if an emergency does come up, you have someone who you can trust to take your dog to. I will go into more about choosing a vet in the next chapter.

YORKIE PROOFING YOUR HOUSE & YARD

You will be amazed at your new Yorkie's unerring ability to find anything and everything around your house that can be sniffed, chewed, dragged, pulled down from counters, and generally destroyed all in the name of curiosity and fun. So, the best thing you can do for your own mental health and the health of your new family member is to go through your house *before* the new arrival hits and make sure house and yard are what I call "Yorkie-proof."

Kitchen

Those counters look high enough, but beware anything that your determined scamp will find to jump up on. I have seen many a Yorkie deduce how to jump from a stool to a counter just because they smell something on the top of the counter that seems interesting.

Agile paws and determined muzzles will poke a cupboard open or scrape something off that might be hanging over the edge. If you are storing solvents or cleaning agents underneath your sink, you may consider installing child locks on those particular doors. Sounds a little paranoid, but believe me, when you picture yourself rushing to the vet only because your little friend opened the door...well, let's just say it's worth the few dollars for the lock.

Even the most refined Yorkie can't resist the tantalizing aroma coming from the garbage can. So pick one that has a secure lid or better yet, keep your garbage in a secure cabinet. And those kitchen towels hanging on a rod to dry may have just enough food smell on them that your clever one may pull them down to investigate.

I always throw away the twist ties off of bread products because I have had Yorkies chew and swallow them. Use a large clip to close bags instead. The same goes for the ties that come with garbage bags.

Not least of all is the *food* that you have in the kitchen. Generally, you will not want your Yorkie eating what you have eaten, whether this is something that was in the garbage or is lying innocently on the counter. Some things like chocolate and chicken bones are quite literally dangerous to Yorkies. Wipe up spills promptly. This is not a breed that cleans kitchen floors without some gastro-intestinal consequence later.

Bathroom

Here, like the kitchen, all kinds of interesting odors reside, just waiting to be checked out. If you keep cleaning powders, like Comet or Ajax, soaps, or shampoos in cupboards or at knee level, consider moving them to a secure location. As intelligent as Yorkies are, they don't always know what will make them sick and you don't want to invite a situation where they have swallowed something and you don't find out until it's too late.

Other things in the bathroom to watch out for are

sanitary napkins and tampons. These are a problem because if they are chewed on and swallowed, your Yorkie's intestinal tract could become obstructed, causing her great pain and possibly death. Watch your bathroom trash can for this and other potential hazards like floss, used toilet paper rolls, medicine bottles with unused medicine inside, etc. Q-tips and emery boards are particular favorites since they are small and easy to carry.

Living Room/Den

This is often a place where you do hobbies and other material-oriented activities. So, if I were a Yorkie, what would I find? I bet I would find paints and brushes from that sunset you were trying to capture this morning. I might also see some knitting or sewing yarn and needles that you left on the sofa when you ran to grab the telephone. And what about that flat board with all those strange shaped pieces on top? That looks like it would make for some good chewing!

The best way to remedy all these hobby hazards is to have a place for the items involved. Do you knit? Keep a knitting bag instead of an open basket. A budding painter? Paint a wooden bin and keep all your creative juices inside. Does that game of chess or checkers seem to go on and on? Better to elevate that to some shelf for now.

Another thing to watch out for, especially if you or someone in your family smokes, is cigarettes and the accompanying ashes. Now ashes and butts aren't the first things most of us think of when we are hungry, but what about a Yorkie that is left home for a few hours? Bored and lonely, the dog might chew cigarettes up just for chewing sake. Empty ashtrays regularly and keep packs of cigarettes in a drawer. Remember, your chewing wonder can also chew through cardboard, no problem. That means chewing tobacco—like the kind that comes in round cardboard tins—also needs to be stored in a drawer or high cupboard.

Are there cords winding around your living room or den like snakes? A friend had a Yorkie puppy that was six months old named Calamity. And she sure lived up to her name at first. She chewed through an electric cord that was plugged in and gave herself severe burns on the inside of her mouth. Luckily, she did survive, but there are a few ways to handle this and avoid such a disaster.

You may see things advertised that you can put on wood and other things called "bitter apple." This may work for a little while, but it's really not a long-term solution. Instead, coil cords up and tuck them out of the way or situate lamps in such a way that the cords don't present such an obvious invitation. And don't worry. You won't have to decorate your house around your Yorkie's whims forever; this is usually just a puppy phase and should pass in a reasonable amount of time.

Bedrooms

At first, your bedroom is probably not the most ideal place for your new arrival. If it's a puppy, she should first get used to sleeping through the night in her own area. If it's an adult, until she becomes accustomed to your nighttime routine, she might use that time to explore.

Your bedroom presents all kinds of interesting things

to chew and sniff. What is wonderful as far as your Yorkie is concerned is that everything has your scent on it! You most likely don't want your clothes chewed on in general anyway, but especially avoid letting your nylons be chewed on. This is another intestinal threat and one that's easy to avoid.

A medication that you take either daily or before bed should *never* be left on your nightstand or a table within the jumping or standing reach of your Yorkie. The same thing goes for any jewelry or coins. It's small and easy to swallow—and a *nightmare* at the vet's! So put it in a jewelry box or a coin box!

For those of you with children, be sure that toys are picked up. Many children's toys will look just like dog toys to a Yorkie, but won't hold up as well.

General House-Proofing

Keep in mind a Yorkie is small and fast, but can't always wriggle out of every sticky situation. Do you have a door in your house that is on a spring or tends to creep shut of its own accord? A Yorkie distracted by following you or playing might be caught in the door and be hurt. Buy a simple rubber door-stop and jam it in the door. If you are going to be going in and out, for instance, of your garage and the door leading into the garage

61

swings shut by itself, you might think about corralling that Yorkie in a safe area until you are through.

Also, watch behind you when you close doors. Your Yorkie will follow you *everywhere* and it is not unusual for her to get left behind when you retreat from the room you were in. Then you will be frantic looking for her and she can't just say, "hey dummy, you locked me in the bedroom!" The same goes for open cupboards at floor level. They're curious and they'll get shut inside that cupboard if you get distracted.

Garage

Most of us have some sort of ongoing project in our garage. That means there will invariably be screws or nails that find their way to the floor. Or if you're into wood projects, it can be tough to get all the wood shavings up from the floor. My suggestion would be to organize your nails and screws in little drawers or boxes

and sweep or use a hand vacuum after a project. Your Yorkie is going to want to be with you all the time since they have a natural curiosity about all that you do. So you want her to be as safe as possible.

The garage is also a likely place for storing things like insecticide, fertilizer, and other poisons. If you park your car in the garage, be particularly mindful of oil or antifreeze leaking from the transmission. Antifreeze smells sweet and by the time you find out your Yorkie has swallowed some, it may be too late.

If you have mouse traps or ant bait lying around in the garage, this is also a threat to your Yorkie. Last but not least, you invariably track things in on your shoes as you re-enter your house. Should you feel that changing the above things is not realistic, the best alternative is to ban your Yorkie from the garage altogether.

Garden & Yard

We have all seen dogs eat grass and we know they do it to help their tummies. But what if you just sprayed fertilizer on that grass? Or what if you have gophers that you are trying to get rid of? You can't very well just pitch gopher poison down a hole and not expect it to arouse the curiosity of your Yorkie. If you need to spray, keep your Yorkie away from the area for at least a few days. This goes for having to spray for spiders, etc. around the perimeter of your house. I recommend that you hire a professional exterminator and tell them you have toy dogs. I have my buildings sprayed twice a year inside and out.

Summer Peril

One summer day years ago I came into the house after working on a sick calf. I sat down and as I looked down the hallway I saw my beautiful Brutus dragging himself toward me. He just couldn't make it and he collapsed. I ran to him as I screamed for someone to call the vet. The first veterinarian didn't answer (it was a Sunday of course), so I said to call another.

Brutus just lay in my arms and I knew he was dying! He felt cold and limp, and even though his eyes were open, he just stared ahead. He couldn't even lift his head. It was all he could do to get halfway down the hall when he had heard my voice before he fell over.

The second veterinarian agreed to meet us at his office and I urged him to hurry, as Brutus was terribly ill. I was trying to keep from falling apart since Brutus was my first Yorkie and I loved him so. I'd had him since he was six days old, when I agreed to babysit him and his adopted mother, a toy poodle. He was my shadow, and truly, my kindred soul. He just couldn't die!

The vet examined him and told me he didn't have much chance. He asked if I had any idea what was wrong. Had he fallen or been injured? I said, "No." Brutus was going into shock so the vet started him on IV's immediately. The veterinarian took Brutus from me and went into the back treatment room while I prayed. Brutus only weighed three and three-quarter pounds at that time and had never been away from me. He seemed so small. The vet saw how broken-hearted I was, so, in a few minutes, he said I could go back where the dogs were kept, and see for myself that Brutus was able to sit up now that he was on an IV. The vet let us leave his blanket with him in his cage.

The vet said he'd run blood tests in the morning, but he didn't want to get my hopes up. He called me later that night to say that Brutus was hanging on. I didn't sleep at all that night. I couldn't figure out what was wrong. Brutus was only a year and a half, had always been healthy and I was just starting what looked to be a promising show career.

The next day my vet called me to say Brutus was improving slightly, as he was no longer in shock, but was still very ill. The lab work would be back later that afternoon. When the vet called back with the lab results, I was really puzzled. He said that Brutus had terrible liver damage. The vet asked if Brutus could have gotten into some poison. I couldn't think of what he could have eaten to make him so sick. Then it hit me. The night before he became ill, a huge green grasshopper had flown

64

into the house through the front door.

As the rest of the family was asleep, and I hate bugs, I got the RAID insecticide and sprayed the grasshopper. Then Brutus and I went to bed. Apparently he'd eaten the grasshopper the next morning before I got up and had ingested a lethal dose of poison. I had actually poisoned my precious Brutus myself.

It was a week before Brutus could come home. He had been on IVs for seven days. By then he was holding his own. I'm so very grateful to a dedicated vet who saw us through this, and I hope that other dog owners will benefit from my close call. I don't allow any insecticides in my house now and I'm especially careful with disinfectants.

Plants, inside your house and out, need to be out of the way of your Yorkie. Hanging plants and plants on windowsills are okay, but use caution about plants that you keep within doggy reach. Be sure to refer to the appendix in the back of this book for a complete list of poisonous plants. Become familiar with this list so that you will never compromise the life of your Yorkie.

Sticks are a favorite find from the yard and your Yorkie may proudly drag one (usually twice her size) into the house to chew on comfortably. But the splinters from a chewed one can perforate the mouth, throat or intestine. Best to distract your stick-finding explorer with some safe chewing like nylabones or floss bones. These will also be good for her teeth.

WHAT DOES YOUR GARDEN GROW?

I remember one summer was a nightmare in terms of a battle that I never quite won. I got some wood chips to accent my flower garden and didn't realize that the wood chips were contaminated with not only Giardia, but also slimy little slugs. Ugh! These two problems began to take over my life.

First we tried to clear up the Giardia with the usual antibiotics, namely Keflex. Unfortunately, three out of four of our Yorkies had a severe reaction to the Keflex and started vomiting. This was on top of the vomiting that was brought on by the Giardia. Since they also had diarrhea, dehydration was a serious consequence to this whole situation. The symptoms seemed to start with a lack of appetite, then vomiting and diarrhea.

We determined that the problem was Giardia by taking a stool sample immediately to the veterinarian for a test that is done in house. We put the sample in double plastic bags, because oxygen seems to stop the detection of Giardia. An old stool would be of little help.

Once we discovered that we couldn't use the Keflex, my veterinarian went to a cattle wormer called Albendazole. We used it at a dose of 1/10 of a cc. per pound of body weight. So a five pound dog would get 5/10 of a cc. twice a day by mouth. This is used for only two days for a total of four doses. We did not use it on puppies under five months old or pregnant bitches. I believe we used the Keflex and Clavamox for them.

I finally put the problem together when I noticed that the dogs would go out into the yard and dig around for a choice piece of chipped wood, chew on it and fight over it. Sure as the world, within two days that dog would have Giardia again. Then the problem of the slugs continued. Since the poison for these slugs is not safe for pets, the only organic cure was to take stale beer and put it in pie pans put into the ground so that the rim was accessible to the slugs, and leave it out at night. The slugs love the taste of the beer, drink it, fall in and drown. Yes, I know it sounds ridiculous, but my local pest control expert suggested it. Since I have Yorkies as well as rare finches, I am doubly careful about using toxic treatments for anything.

The only success that I had was using bleach in a spray applicator that attaches to the water hose to try to combat the slugs but I had to repeat it several times. It slowed down the slugs, but certainly not enough. I finally got rid of the Giardia by making a liquid medicine for the Yorkies from the human antibiotic, Ciprofloxacin (sister drug to Batril).

I finally decided to sell the house and move; it was the only answer. I did not take any of my bulbs or rose bushes from this yard to my next yard. I will not be using wood chips in my new yard either and I will use bleach to clean my lawn mower before I use it on my new lawn. What a mess!

Fence Security

Before your new Yorkie even arrives, it is a good idea to walk your yard and examine your fence. Is it securely in the ground? Are there holes and gaps? Are there areas of dirt that have become sinkholes from the weather, enough for a small animal to squeeze through? A Yorkie can fit in and through a smaller space than you can imagine, so if you have any of the above problems mending your fence may be in order.

If there is any question about the security of your fence and you want your Yorkie to spend time outside, you may want to invest in an exercise pen. Usually made of metal, they are available in various sizes and assemble easily to create a safe area for your Yorkie to play or rest in outside. These are ideal for travel and when company comes to visit, especially if there are people coming in and out of the house frequently.

Decks and Stairs

Decks with wide slats in them and flights of stairs with open boarding can be treacherous for a dog as small as a Yorkie. You may elect to buy a wire dog fence, which can be attached easily with nails to your wood deck and set a boundary against stairs or other hazards that way.

If your deck has wide slats of wood where the dog can poke its head through, it may be time to get creative there as well. You can get a fine chicken wire that will be inexpensive, protective and unobtrusive at the same time. I would say that most of the time, a Yorkie has a good enough sense of heights, but should the dog lose her balance for any reason—for example, if you or something else comes up behind her and startles her—then she could fall and be severely injured or killed.

Open stairs, where there are wide spaces underneath the top of each stair, can present a problem, too, especially for a smaller Yorkie. Consider that Yorkies are sometimes only a smattering of inches in height and the very act of going up stairs that are the same height as they are can be a challenge. What I did for one of my Yorkies, Thadius, was to buy a plank of wood the length of the flight of stairs and nail it to the stairs. Then I put rubber strips down and short pieces of wood like a ladder down the length of wood for grip and slipping. He went up and down that plank of wood like crazy and it saved injuries to his legs. So that may be an option for little dogs or for all Yorkies.

Pool/Spa

On sunny days, it is tempting to lay out in the sun by our backyard pool and enjoy the company of our favorite friend. But keep in mind that although Yorkies can swim, they cannot easily climb out of a pool they fall into. Never leave your Yorkie unattended by your pool or spa. The sides are too steep and if the dog swims until the point of exhaustion, she will eventually just give up and drown unless you happen to rescue her. If you have to run inside to answer the front door or pick up the ringing phone, take your Yorkie with you.

To avoid this problem at one house, I installed a fine mesh fence 24 inches high before I even moved in. That way there was no question of whether we had Yorkies by the pool or not. Remember pools attract bees and wasps as well and that can be another hazard.

Pool Story

A lady I knew once had a Yorkie named Candy. Candy was as sweet as her name implied and she was a real people person. She loved to be where the action was. This lady let her two dogs out and went over to a friend's house. When she returned, she remembered she had not brought the dogs in and it had started to rain. Then her friend brought Candy into the house soaking wet and said, "She's gone." She figured out that even though the pool was covered, Candy had slipped walking near the edge and she could not pull herself out of the pool. It was such a tragedy for this lady; it was unbearable for her to imagine what must have been going through Candy's mind as she struggled for her life in the water.

The same thing that happened to Candy could happen to your little treasure so beware! You may even go so far as to block off the areas of water like I did or not let your Yorkie outside if there is a pool. Dogs are fascinated by water so you are the only one that can keep them safe.

Caution Out of the Wind

Preparing your house and yard will only serve to make you more aware of the hazards around you and also awaken you to the possibilities of what your new arrival may discover. Toy dogs are really "hot house flowers" in the sense that they cannot exist without the human support and the greenhouse environment that you provide them. There are many pitfalls in this big world for tiny little dogs. If you want to have your toy dog for a long time, you need to be aware of them and protect your Yorkie from some of the perils that are out there—in the world and in their own house.

Chapter 4

Choosing a Vet

As I said in the previous chapter, begin researching what veterinarian you will bring your Yorkie to *before* he or she arrives. Yorkies are different than most dogs because they are toys and cannot be treated the same as a larger dog, like a St Bernard. Therefore, you are looking for a vet that might even be a specialist in toy dogs or simply sees a lot of them and has experience dealing with the special crises that can arise. At any rate, you need someone that you feel comfortable with and that you will be able to trust with the life of your Yorkie.

How to Find a Vet

You may have other pets in the house (not Yorkies) that you have a vet for. And perhaps you feel that your vet is competent enough to deal with your Yorkie. Otherwise, you may look for a vet especially for your Yorkie.

If you know someone in your area that has Yorkies or other toy dogs, you may ask them for a referral. Ask them why they like a certain vet and see if that might be what you are looking for, too.

If you just moved to the area or don't know anyone with Yorkies, you will have to take the long road: the yellow pages. Before randomly picking a name, try calling your local kennel club if there is one. Local groomers may also have advice about the preferred vets in town.

You may end up calling a few vets just to see how comfortable you are with them. When I move to a new town, I take a day and make appointments with all the best vets. I don't take a dog with me. I am so concerned about the welfare of my Yorkies that I am willing to pay for an office visit just to interview the vet. This way you can make sure you have a good match for you and your Yorkie's needs.

Large Clinics vs. Small Practices

Does the staff seem friendly and helpful? Do they seem overworked? I have found that in offices where they have a lot of business, things can seem harried at times. This tells me that they are probably reputable and competent; however, be prepared to wait and most likely have your vet run late much of the time. You may not feel comfortable in this kind of setting. Of course, what I call "country" vets are becoming more and more rare. These are the types of vets who operate out of small offices and who are easily accessible to their clients, pretty much any time.

The large clinic has 7 day a week 24-hour service most of the time, while a small, independent office might refer all after-hours calls to a local emergency clinic. My preference would be the large clinic since most emergencies seem to happen either at night, on the weekends, or on holidays.

Also if there are five or six vets, I try to choose two and become familiar with them. Preferably I like them and can communicate with them. Then I request my appointments to be with one of the two (whoever is available) so that they come to know me and know my dogs. This is possibly another reason to look for a larger clinic so you have a choice.

What to Ask

Don't be afraid to ask a lot of questions. When does this clinic or office open in the morning? How late are they open? Are they by appointment only or is there a day during the week that they accept walk-ins? What are their holiday hours? Do they have emergency hours? Are emergencies handled by one of their vets or do they refer clients to a local emergency clinic that all local vets refer to?

Referrals to Specialist

Another important issue that we all hope we don't have to deal with (but you might someday) is that of bringing your Yorkie to a specialist. If you are faced with some sort of surgery, you may be pointed in the direction of a specialist. Sometimes the specialist might

73

be hundreds of miles away in another state. These specialists have equipment that is not normally available to the average vet as well as doctors skilled in using them.

One time a Yorkie had a fractured tooth that needed a root canal. It was 250 miles to the facility where this procedure could be done. But at least I knew we would be in experienced, competent hands that my local vet had no trouble referring us to.

I encourage you to ask your general vet about what specialists he or she would refer you to. In this way, you will know whether your vet is objective about what areas he or she is strong in and what areas he or she would feel more comfortable referring you to someone else. After all, if your Yorkie has a special need, you don't want the pride of someone who thinks that they know it all and can handle it all; you want the best person for the job.

Knowledge of Yorkies

Toy dogs have different life challenges than their larger dog counterparts. That's why I personally feel best with a veterinarian who is knowledgeable about

Yorkies to such an extent that they have kept up to date on problems typical to the breed. For instance, you would want your vet to be able to tell you that toy breeds, such as Yorkies, inherently have dental (teeth, gums, and bones) problems. Or that they have had liver shunt or L'egg

Perthes in the breed. You want to be comfortable with his knowledge of the breed because then you will feel comfortable about how he treats your Yorkie medically.

I am fortunate enough to have a vet who is willing to make house calls and always takes my dog home with him if an overnight stay is required. A Yorkie should never be left in the office to be checked in the morning. Depending on the situation, they could take a turn for the worse during the night and there would be no one there who could truly help the dog. You also don't want your Yorkie to be left alone because they are so dependent on you that they might think they have been abandoned, and give up hope and die. There is not much grey area to work with when it comes to a Yorkie.

The Teeth Issue

About 15 years ago, I noticed that my Yorkies started losing all their teeth by about three and four years old. Too young, I thought. I would boil beef rib bones for them to chew on, because I thought that it might be caused by lack of circulation to the jawbones due to insufficient chewing.

On one occasion, I spoke to the technician who was cleaning my dogs' teeth. He was describing this new tool that used high speed, ultrasonic vibrations to chip the tartar away from teeth. He complained that any variation in speed or direction of the tool was disastrous and that the tool was very prone to needing tuning.

A couple of years of cleaning my dogs' teeth a few times a year with this tool and all my dogs were almost toothless, at least as far as the smaller teeth.

And despite the supposed advanced technology of this tool, they not only developed gum disease, but each time they went in for cleaning, they would lose more teeth. Ironically, the dogs that went in more often to try to control their problems got worse results.

After about three years of having my dogs' teeth cleaned with the ultrasound equipment, I realized the problem. Since the teeth were so small, they were being chipped away from the bones by the vibrations just like tartar on large dogs' teeth, and subsequently the tooth would actually die. Then six months later, when I returned for another cleaning, we'd lose more teeth. The gum disease would get increasingly worse with every cleaning.

All my Yorkies that had their teeth cleaned with the ultrasonic tool lost most of their teeth by age three. This wasn't surprising since the teeth were dying each time the ultrasonic vibrations loosened them from the bones.

Our top-producing bitch at the time had beautiful teeth and gums, had her teeth scaled by hand and didn't lose any teeth until after she was eight years of age. At age 13, she still has all her teeth (except that one) and so does her daughter (10) and son (9).

Why Clean the Teeth at all Then?

By now you're probably wondering, why go through the teeth cleaning process? Can't I take good enough care of my Yorkie's teeth at home? The answer is strikingly similar to a human problem: gum disease. Most toy breeders know that the biggest killer of toy dogs is heart and kidney disease caused by gum disease that travels into the bloodstream through the large blood vessels under the tongue, leading directly to the heart. So gum disease is a contributing factor in the eventual loss of the pet.

Overworking the kidneys with toxins and bacteria from bad teeth and gum disease can compromise the animal's ability to handle anesthesia as well as exacerbate any other health problem that is on going at the time. The more often they have to go under anesthesia for teeth cleaning and pulling, the more stress put on their vital organs.

About six or seven years ago I put a stop to it with my dogs. I started requesting the veterinarian to "hand scale only" on my dogs' teeth. This is a much gentler process on the teeth and then when they are buffed they sparkle. Hand scaling does not remove all tartar, but the trace amounts that are left are so minimal that you cannot tell. Since we have been doing this, none of my dogs lose teeth prematurely anymore.

Different vets have different ways of dealing with the actual teeth cleaning process and the anesthesia used. You want to look for a dental specialist or a vet who is willing to hand scale the teeth of your dogs. No matter what, the person must listen to your needs regarding your dog's teeth.

The Process of Getting a Vet to Hand Scale

I don't tell the vet "I want them to hand scale"—I tell them that "I will only allow them to be hand scaled." This can be done nicely but firmly. Call the vet ahead of time and also check out the type of anesthesia used (more on that next). Be prepared for the hand scaling to cost more as well. In fact, you may want to let the vet know that you are prepared to pay more for the extra time. If they say that they will *not* hand scale no matter what, go somewhere else. They should be able to give you answers and options that are agreeable to you.

If the vet is planted firmly in the ground on teeth and anesthesia issues and you are uncomfortable with their answers, you need a different vet. This could be a sign that they are lazy, in a hurry (hand scaling is more time consuming), don't want to bother, or so hung up on their own ego that they can't listen to new ideas. It is a standard part of the procedure to 'polish' the teeth at the end of cleaning with a buffer tool; this cleans the tooth fairly well, including at the gum line, reducing the need to use the ultrasonic tool.

You must take charge and protect the life and dental health of your Yorkie. *That* is why this is an issue in selecting a vet. I go into more detail regarding what *you* can do to maintain healthy Yorkie teeth in Chapter 7.

The Anesthesia Issue

Directly related to the teeth challenge is the question of which anesthesia to use when your Yorkie has to undergo surgical or dental procedures. I can't tell you how many toys are lost to anesthesia complications during simple routine procedures like teeth cleaning, extractions or OFA x-rays.

There are three main gases used routinely. They are Halythaine, Metathaine, and Isofluorine. Isofluorine is the best for most optional procedures since it causes fewer complications to the heart and kidneys and is very quickly "breathed off." Dogs will wake up within moments of stopping the flow of gas.

I learned many years ago, about the time Isofluorine gas became available, that toy dogs can be "masked down" with no trouble. The procedure with the vet I now use is to mask the dog down, place the tube for the anesthetic gas/oxygen in their throat (there throughout the procedure), perform the oral cleaning, and also perform a larynx/pharal cleaning to be sure there is no debris in the throat.

This means that it is unnecessary and *very dangerous* to use any injected anesthetic to induce a state of anesthesia in a Yorkie. It is a simple and much safer procedure to just put the gas mask on the dog and hold it there for a few moments, and they go right under.

What's Wrong with Anesthetic Injections?

Toy dogs are particularly susceptible to negative effects from an injected anesthetic due to the fact that the kidneys must metabolize the drugs in order to get them out of the bloodstream. If the kidneys can't metabolize the drug fast enough, the dog can become toxic and die very quickly. If the injectible is too strong or the dose is too high, there is no way to retrieve it from the bloodstream. Again, the kidneys must clean out the toxin or the dog can die.

The beauty of using gas only is that gases are vaporized out of the lungs and can actually be "pulled out of the lungs" by a method called "bagging" if the dog isn't breathing on its own. A balloon-type apparatus is squeezed by hand, forcing pure oxygen into the dog's lungs. As the carbon dioxide comes out of the dog's lungs and the oxygen goes in, the gas anesthesia comes right out at the same time.

With hand scaling, your Yorkie will be under the anesthesia longer. I would estimate that the average dog would be under for about 15 to 20 minutes using the ultrasonic tool and 35 to 40 minutes hand scaling (depending of course on how much plaque and tartar there is on the teeth). As I said, this may be an issue for your vet, but as far as the way the dog is anesthetized, it is significant that you mask down without an injectible. You can see that you have much more control even if the procedure takes longer.

Once I needed to have a canine tooth pulled on my fourteen and a half year-old Yorkie, "Thadius" and the veterinarian was very cautious due to his age. He didn't even want to put a tube down his throat for the anesthesia, so he just barely gassed him under and worked a few minutes and when Thad would start to come around, he'd hold the gas on a few minutes and out Thad would go. That gave him time to pull the tooth, pack and stitch the gum (an upper canine) and in twenty minutes Thadius was ready to go home.

Facing the Objections

The vet may tell you that it will take too long to use the gas only method and that they want to use an injection *and* the gas. They may tell you that it is because the tube gets in the way when they are cleaning the teeth or because it takes too much effort to constantly monitor the dog's level of anesthesia. If your vet is not willing to work with you, there is another vet out there who will.

If you don't know what your veterinarian is using, you can tell by how quickly the dog is up and on its feet. Just ask how long before you can take your dog home. When gas is used, the dog is ready to go home

80

in half an hour. Injected sedatives or anesthetics will leave the dog groggy and drugged for many hours after they wake up.

Again, *ask* about the method of anesthesia. If the vet will not use gas alone, go to another vet. The way I see it, it's your dog so it's your way—or not at all.

Okay to Ask Questions

How comfortable do you feel when you talk to the vet? Does he or she answer your questions in a way that is not condescending, yet you can understand? Do you feel he or she is open to any questions you may ask about procedures, clinic practices, etc.? Your vet should be able to communicate in such a way that you leave the office knowing that *you* know all the options.

Belle's Story

When we went to a vet for one of my Yorkies, Belle, who had a rattle in her throat, we explained all her symptoms. The vet was a woman who was open and friendly. She was not offended that I was a breeder and wanted detailed information about what was going to happen. Since we were from out of town, I had no experience with this clinic, although we had contacted a local toy breeder and were referred to them.

I had to give Belle medication during the night as she had gotten worse. Since we had no vet to go to, we were stuck until morning until we could get a referral. This vet was not upset that I had treated Belle with medicine and because I could "fess up" to this, it made the interpretation of the test more viable. We did blood work-ups, x-rays, and exams. Still no answers. But the vet was willing to fax the results to me at my office and to my regular vet in Durango, as well as give me the x-rays to give to my vet. As one possibility, we tested for "Valley Fever." I also had her check her liver functions as well as her white count. Everything came back normal and with this information she confirmed that I had given her the right medicine the night before.

After tests and exams (ending up at an ear, nose and throat specialist), no one could tell us what was wrong. And this was after it had been going on from July to February. We had had her flushed inside and out by the specialists. She got worse within three days and finally I knew she would die very soon. I held her in my lap and talked softly to her. She seemed to know it, too, because she stayed close to us.

I reached a point that night where I knew I had to act fast or she would be gone in 24 hours. I call this next decision, "kill or cure." With nothing to lose (we would lose her anyway if I didn't do *something*), I tried a drug used as a human antibiotic called Ciprofloxacin. Mixing it with water for 20 doses, I gave it to her and watched what would happen. I had to trust my instincts and pray that I was doing the right thing.

After ten days (that in itself was a miracle), she showed signs of improving. The rattle from her throat/sinuses was not as loud. I kept this medication up for 20 days and on day 21, Belle was breathing normally and has been fine ever since.

Advice on the Phone

Finally, do you feel that you would be able to get advice from the vet over the phone if your Yorkie had some simple problem or if you just wanted to ask a question? What if you were traveling and needed advice? I believe there has to be a balance between a vet who has you coming in all the time, at the drop of a hat, and an owner who calls incessantly whenever they feel the whim. Your vet should be open to answering questions by phone (they usually set aside a certain amount of their day for callbacks) and you should have the courtesy to know not to take advantage of their generosity and time. It's a fine line, but I think it can exist.

Remember Whose Heart it is

I know this seems like a lot to think about, but you must ask yourself, who owns this Yorkie? Who will be paying the vet bills and suffering the anxiety if things go wrong? Whose emotions will be tightly entwined with this little creature's every movement and action? You need to be a team with you working as a nurse in the field, giving vital information to the vet and following instructions concerning medications at home. If you plan to give your heart to a Yorkie, plan to ensure her life with a competent and approachable veterinarian.

Chapter 5

Training Your Yorkie

Yorkies learn by positive reinforcement, so train them that they can please you by doing certain things and reward them to reinforce the memory in their brain. Because Yorkies are so intelligent, you can begin training them almost immediately.

TRAINING CLASSES

I don't discourage the use of training classes (ones where owner and dog both attend) for Yorkies. I believe that with the intelligence of this breed, they can respond very well to professional guidance. What I will tell you is that unless you attend a class specifically for small or toy dogs, there is the danger that someone else's dog—invariably a *much larger* dog—could get loose and injure or kill your Yorkie. I have seen it happen. I have heard stories from people who brought their Yorkie to a training class and watched helplessly as a large dog broke loose from its owner and picked up their Yorkie in its mouth, shaking it like a rag.

I tell you this not so you can be paranoid or live in constant fear, but so that you can live in awareness that your new friend needs your protection. You need to be aware of what is around you, no matter where you are, when you are out in public with your Yorkie. One unguarded moment is all it would take for tragedy to strike.

Note also that if anything in the class makes you uncomfortable, whether it is the way the instructor handles a dog or speaks to you, don't proceed. What's at stake here is not just your Yorkie's well-being, but also your own frame of mind. I don't want you to ever feel you have been cruel or unjust to your friend because that is the saddest thing I could imagine. This should be rewarding and create a special bond between you and your Yorkie.

Digging in the Dirt

I knew a lady who had a much-beloved little boy Yorkie named Lobo. There was never a more spoiled Yorkie than him.

When they got him, they had a baby shower and all their friends brought him things. He got presents for Christmas and on his birthday.

One day the lady was walking her Yorkie in the park (on a leash) and two huge black labs (*not* on leashes) ran up and attacked him. She picked Lobo up and ran to a neighbor's house and they drove to the vet together. Lobo died on the way.

This perfect, precious puppy that was loved so much was the unwitting victim of someone else's carelessness. The lady could not look anywhere in her home without remembering some Lobo antics and her house was filled with flowers from friends who shared her grief.

You never think that something like this will happen to you. You always hear people tell you "my dog won't bite." They use this as a rationalization for leaving their dog off a leash. Everyone thinks of labs as "America'a favorite dogs" and no one believes that *any* dog is capable of something like this. But they *are*. You cannot control what other people do with their animals, but you can control your own awareness of what is around you. When you are *anywhere* with your Yorkie, you must *constantly* be aware of what is around you. Never let your guard down for one minute. Your dog's life is in your hands.

ROUTINE

Yorkies are very routine-oriented dogs. In other words, if you are used to getting up at 5:30 in the morning, that is okay with them, too. I have even had Yorkies that literally "tell time" because they are so in tune with the part of the day when they are fed or when you return from work. They mold themselves to your life, which is wonderful if you are looking for a constant companion. However, they can also be flexible given the time to get used to a new idea.

For instance, if you are someone who stays at home a lot of the time—perhaps you run your business out of your home—and you are planning a ten-day road trip, it will be a lot easier on both you and your Yorkie if you start ahead of time. In other words, don't just come to the day the trip starts and head out. Take your Yorkie on short trips so that she knows that trips are a part of her life routine. I'll talk more about traveling with Yorkies in chapter 8.

Routine is particularly important when you are training a Yorkie, both in basic commands and in housebreaking. Your consistency will create a consistency in their behavior and you'll have a more obedient Yorkie that will be a pleasure to live with.

YOUR BODY LANGUAGE

You are the "alpha Yorkie" in your house. All the dogs look to you for guidance. If you are handling a Yorkie—for instance to brush teeth or groom coats—and you are hesitant or uncertain, the dog will pick up on that and use it to her advantage. If she knows that every time she cries when you are brushing her hair you will stop, you'll never get anywhere with that brush. So it's important for you to be aware of your position as the head of the house.

Yorkies will bond with different people than may have been planned for so it's a good idea to have more than one person take part in the discipline. In this case, there can be more than one alpha dog—you and your husband or whatever. This is necessary because if you are gone for any length of time, the dog may react by suddenly becoming lax in her house training or by chewing forbidden items. I have had dogs that refused to eat if I left on a trip without them. I have learned to try and encourage flexibility and adaptability so that change isn't as traumatic.

What Body Language Should I Use?

Your Yorkie will read you like a book, constantly tuning into your body language, expressions on your face, etc. *Never hit, yell or yank* the harness of your Yorkie—trust me, they will never forget it if you do. From the beginning, it is your body language that will instill a lifetime of trust or alienate your new companion forever.

Voice

Of all the means of communication you can use, your voice is the most powerful. How your voice sounds will determine the attitude of your Yorkie toward you *and* whether she is likely to respond to you positively or negatively. The tone of your voice is crucial to what you want your Yorkie to do. When you are excited and have a high, upbeat tone when you praise her, then she will always associate that with happiness and good things. You can switch the tone of your voice to a deep, lower tone to emphasize the authority of your commands and to let her know her accident on the floor is not acceptable. Your Yorkie will quickly recognize repetition of words or phrases with the same tone of voice.

Attitude

If you are training and your Yorkie is not responding immediately, it is better to keep trying with a good attitude. Don't forget a treat when she does even the smallest thing right. If you are exhausted by your efforts, the dog probably is, too, so try another time. Avoid getting angry with her because that will only affect the rest of the training session. Yorkies are so in tune with their person that they sense your disappointment or anger and will respond in kind. For instance, a dog that knows your anger over potty accidents can respond by cowering or hiding in a corner or against the wall.

Sometimes moving on to another lesson and in effect changing the subject can refresh the energy of teaching your Yorkie. When she is engrossed in the new task, you can come back to the one from before and it will be easier to accomplish.

Your training with basic commands can be instrumental in achieving your alpha dog status. If you are lead training, be sure that your Yorkie learns to come to you and be still so you can easily put the lead on. If you have a beggar around your own meal times, don't give in to the urge to throw her scraps or to stop your own meal and feed her first. And be consistent. Don't ignore your training and commands just because you have guests over or you'll send a clear message that guests mean your Yorkie can be a bad actor.

If you teach your Yorkie that it is acceptable to roll on her back on the ground for a tummy rub, be prepared for her to do it *every time* you go to pet or pick her up. You may choose to only allow her to lay on her back when she is in your lap or on furniture.

If your dog already has this behavior or if you want to prevent it, start ignoring this response. If she rolls on her back, walk away and when she gets up, praise her for that. When you're sitting in a chair, get her to come to you and through repetition, you get her to allow you to pat her on the back. Pat her one or two time, combined with the praise. This is a process of retraining the thinking inside their head.

Next step in training your Yorkie to be picked up, use a lead, and reach down and pick her up while she is still on her feet. Praise her for staying on her feet, but if she rolls on her back, walk away and start over. This is an example of how it is easier to teach good habits from the beginning instead of trying to undo bad habits later.

Know Who's in Charge

The best thing you can do for your own benefit and that of your little friend is to set your boundaries right away. Make your "No's" loud and clear. Be realistic about what you expect for the long term. Remember you can be in charge without being overly forceful or abusive. Overall, your attitude and thus your body language should convey a balance between harsh punishment (which will *not* win the trust of your Yorkie) and excessive freedom (in which case you'll be a crazy person).

PICKING UP A YORKIE

Toy dogs need to be held differently. I learned this from a Chihuahua breeder about 15 years ago. He demonstrated how one hand should be under the dogs' ribs, fingers spread, and the second hand should be over the top of the dog's back, fingers and thumb encasing the neck. This forms a body hold on both top and bottom. The reason for this is that Yorkies are unusually energetic and animated even in mid air. They can put their hind feet up on your arm and catapult or springboard off your arm or body right out of your hands. If you hold the dog close to your body as I described above, she will not be able to launch herself.

Once you have the dog up, if she becomes unbalanced or tries to jump down, grab the hair under the chest and between the front legs to keep her from escaping your grasp. For safety's sake, you may want to incorporate this into the way you hold your Yorkie.

If you need to carry the dog, hold her snugly between the support hand and your body. When you go to put her down or hand her to someone, move the other hand over the top of the rib area to stabilize her once she is away from your body. Never try to lift or hand off with one hand.

On one occasion one of our own dogs was being handed from one person to another to go outside a motor home to go potty, and was being picked up with each hand on one side of the dog. He jumped his hind feet off of the tummy of his mom and went flying out of her hands. As he came down he hit his head on a heater and broke his neck. He was a lovely four-year old champion named Lemire's Goodpuppy Gambit.

Another mistake that a friend of mine made was to carry her Yorkie in her arms (arms crossed in front of her chest). Chelsey decided to get down and jumped right off onto the rock patio. She broke her pelvis and her mom's heart, but lived to tell about it.

HANDLING

Your Yorkie should be used to being picked up and handled on all parts of her body. In the course of her life, she will have teeth brushed, coat groomed, eyes cleaned, etc. and shouldn't be entirely shy about being handled. The best way to accustom her to this is to touch her from nose to toe frequently. I teach my dogs to lay in my lap on their backs from the time they are puppies. There are so many things that are easier to do if they just relax on their backs. All this will take is time, patience and consistency.

For instance almost *no* dog likes its toenails or feet touched, but if you start from the time they are very young, you can overcome this dislike. Including her toes in various favorite massages like belly rubs can reassure your Yorkie that no harm will come to her there. Constant touching will build up a bond of trust between you and your Yorkie and get her used to the kind of handling she will experience all her life. I'll tell you more about the right ways to address grooming issues in chapter 7.

TOYS

Puppies that have the right toys will be less likely to be destructive, develop more physically, and have a better chance of losing puppy (deciduous) teeth quickly.

One of the best chewing toys I have seen is made by Nylabone. It comes in three sizes, and is covered with little stipples or projecting pieces of rubber. This is especially helpful for active chewers because it does wonders for their dental health. A Yorkie considers a brand new chew bone a challenge. If you have two Yorkies, be sure to buy one for each of them;

then watch the fun begin. Two Yorkies who are half sisters and get along wonderfully have an animated game of getting the other one's toy. No matter what, they want what the other one has!

Cow hooves, pig ears and rawhide chews are all pure protein. Although the dogs love them, they can cause diarrhea and throw their body's protein level out of control, sometimes permanently. They will also make your Yorkie's breath smell like she has just eaten manure, so I would definitely avoid them.

USING TREATS, TOYS & PRAISE

There are a number of ways you can incorporate positive reinforcement into your training. What is your Yorkie motivated by? You'll find out quickly enough after you try any one of these methods.

Food

Dogs love food—that's a fact. And Yorkies are no exception. Food can be a positive alternative to stern correction in some cases. If you want your Yorkie to drop something she is chewing on (like a shoe), try tempting her with a doggy biscuit or Nylabone. I guarantee that after a few times of seeing that when you call her, you have something good to eat, she will respond more quickly to your calling voice. In this way you avoid bad behavior and your Yorkie is happy, too.

Toys

Another way of distracting your Yorkie from bad behavior is introducing a new toy—whether it's a ball, a chew chip or a chew bone. If you have a dog that loves to chew and she has just obeyed a command to sit, give her a treat that will last for a while. Again, this is a simple and positive way of achieving good behavior and it keeps her busy for a while and keeps your mind at ease.

Praise/Attention

Praise from you is the one thing that most all Yorkies will respond to. Tell your Yorkie what a good girl she is, in an upbeat voice, and she will glow. Petting or scratching behind the ears makes being good while getting their toenails clipped or sitting and staying worthwhile. Giving her your complete attention is like paradise for your Yorkie.

HOUSEBREAKING

Housebreaking is generally the most pressing issue for anyone with a new Yorkie. Do your best as doggie mommy (or daddy) to set your new arrival up for success. How can you do this? To start with, when you bring a puppy home, I strongly advise that you keep her confined in small areas of the house at first rather than allowing her to run all over. Not only will you have more control of where she has accidents (and she will), but it is overwhelming for your Yorkie to have this huge space presented to her. You will make sure she feels comfortable with her surroundings a little at a time and you'll be rewarded by a more confident Yorkie.

What Are Your Circumstances?

One of the joys of Yorkies is the ability to have them in small spaces like apartments. It is likely that apartment dwellers will have a different way of housebreaking than house dwellers. Do you live in a studio apartment in a high rise building on the 21st floor? With the small amount of space and inconvenience of taking potty runs, you will want to paper train or pee pad train your new arrival.

In addition, if you are a senior you may not be as mobile as you used to be. Therefore, you will want your Yorkie to be as self-sufficient as possible and that is another good reason to paper train either puppies or adults.

I live in areas of high altitude and lots of snow and blistering cold weather. Houses are built on a foundation with steps up to the door frame. So turning a puppy loose to fall down the steps or get soaked in freezing rain is unrealistic. We have had snow accumulations of up to 50 inches and have to blaze a trail through the snow and carry our dogs down to it. If you live in the desert where temperatures are 110 degrees and the ground is so hot that it would burn the puppy's pads, you need another option.

If you live in a small apartment where you would have to get dressed at midnight and take your puppy outside and walk it at night by yourself and you are afraid because of the security factor, you need another way to deal with the "potty dilemma." We travel a lot and stay in motels. If I have a dog whining to go outside at 2:00 am, I'm not about to go outdoors with a dog by myself.

All of this brings me to paper training. Remember, it is a natural instinct for dogs to potty outside so you can always train them to do that later (for instance, if you move to a place with a yard or a more temperate climate). Teaching them to go on paper is a bit of a trick, but ideally you would want them to do both depending on the circumstances.

Paper Method

I start teaching my puppies to use paper from the moment they learn to wiggle out of the nest. I don't use newspaper; I use unprinted newspaper end rolls because it doesn't mess up the floor it's on and newspaper can result in dirty paws and a terrible smell from the ink and urine combining. Another suggestion is to use butcher paper that also comes in rolls from art supply stores. I line all the cages and x-pens (otherwise known as exercise pens) with this paper so completely that they cannot miss it even if they try. This establishes a memory of using this paper almost from the beginning.

Spread the paper in a designated area, but be sure you have a vinyl or plastic sheet underneath to shield the carpet or floor. Leave a soiled sheet of paper on top so the scent will make it obvious that this is an okay place to go.

Running Errands & Traveling: the Paper Advantage

When I have to leave home, I always put the dogs in pens lined with several layers of the paper. Lay this on linoleum or vinyl floors so that even if they soak through the worst that happens is you have to mop the floor.

Another advantage of paper training is how easy it is when you are traveling. I take the paper (large sheets that are folded and packed) and a rolled up piece of vinyl to put under the paper and exercise pen. This protects the floors and carpets in the motel rooms and the motor home. Take large plastic bags to roll up soiled papers and throw them away, so that the room is clean and tidy when you leave. Most likely you might need to stay there again sometime and you want to be welcome.

We stay at many motels and if they disclose that pets are not welcome, we go somewhere else. But if there is no sign saying they are not allowed we stay and do not tell them about the dogs. When we leave we always make sure the room is clean and unsoiled so that they do not even know we had dogs with us. Paper training is one of the best ways to leave things the way you would want them left.

Pee Pads

You can find what are called "pee pads" at the grocery store. The advantage to pee pads is that they are imbued with a special scent to invite puppies to pee on them. The only drawback I have found is that rambunctious puppies tend to think this is a toy lying on the ground and shred it to pieces. So then not only do you not get the point across, but you also have to spend time cleaning up bits of paper and plastic. It's also dangerous for your Yorkie to swallow any of these pieces as they are similar materials that diapers are made of.

Pee pads are possible to use once the Yorkie is grown up enough to not want to shred them just for the fun of it. They might be ideal for a rescue Yorkie or for younger adult dog just coming into your house. You also may prefer the convenience of their size and the ease of their availability over the layers of paper. But if you notice that your Yorkie, puppy or adult, is chewing on them, it's over for the pee pad method.

Crate Training

Most dogs will not soil the area where they sleep and Yorkies especially love to be clean and tidy. That is why a crate is one ideal way of not only creating a housebreaking routine, but also letting your Yorkie have a place all her own.

Buy a crate that is made of metal or plastic, not wide enough for small heads to poke through, and is just big enough for your dog to stand up and turn around in. Any bigger and your Yorkie will have room to pee in one corner and sleep in the other.

Introducing her to the crate is an important part of how she will feel about being inside what to her is at first a strange and possibly daunting metal cage. Set the crate on the floor gently and open the door. Don't thrust your Yorkie inside and slam the door behind her; this is no way to build trust. Instead try tempting her inside with a few biscuits and let her explore the crate on her own terms. Kind praise and encouragement works wonders here. If she goes inside, tell her what a good girl she is. Repeat the biscuit act a few times until she goes in and out on her own.

Once she has gotten over her initial apprehension of this metal creature, you can try closing the door with her inside. Again, lots of praise. You can also keep her company with toys and a blanket, which are not only comforting but also emphasize that the crate is not a potty place.

The crate is also not a place to put your Yorkie for punishment. It *is* a safe place to keep puppy safe from big feet that might step on her. The association with the crate should be one of safety and security, a place to go when the world gets a little too big.

Your Rescue Yorkie & Crate Training

If you have a rescue Yorkie, she probably has no training or inhibitions about using her crate to go potty. Training her will be much more difficult. Keeping her and her bedding very clean all the time will differentiate between being in clean surroundings and living in a soiled environment. Hopefully, the canine instinct to avoid soiling her nest or bedding will take over and the training can begin.

In any case, lots of praise for doing her business in the right place helps to reinforce this as a positive act; therefore she will want to repeat this to please you. Take her outside often to give her many chances to succeed.

Preventing Accidents

Besides keeping your Yorkie in sight at all times, which can cut down on the number of bad potties, you can regulate the food and water schedule so that her bladder will be controlled more naturally.

I try to ignore the mishaps that I don't catch and clean them up right away to help the Yorkie learn to live in a clean home. Animals usually go to the same spot to do their business over and over. And, I've found that they usually have one place for peeing and another for pooing. I like the word to go 'poo' instead of 'pooping.' It has a nicer, more natural sound to me, so in this writing this is the word I'll continue to use.

Once the dog moves into larger spaces such as giving them access to using a whole room instead of just an x-pen, or perhaps is allowed to have the run of the house, you need to watch to see where they go to repeatedly to pee or poo. That is where you need to put the paper. Don't try to get them to like the spot you pick out, but rather put the paper in the spot they pick out. They will continue to go back to it, whether you put paper there or not.

Then if you save a layer of paper that has their scent when you change paper and put it on top of the clean papers, you will encourage them to return to the same spot. This is what I mean by setting them up to succeed.

Disciplining Potty Accidents

And yes, accidents *will* happen so expect them. These are little dogs we're talking about here, so the space in their bladders is at a premium. The best rule of thumb is that if you don't catch them in the act, there's no way that punishing them is going to make a difference for the next time.

If you catch your darling angel in the act of piddling, you obviously want to stop her. So creating some noise can help. I say, "huh, huh," and "no" in a low, firm tone of voice. I even ask my Yorkie, "what are you doing?" I praise her as I put her on the paper so that she knows *this* is what pleases me.

In case it's not already obvious, let me say it now. Yorkies have long memories. You should never yell at her or hit her with your hand or any other object. Believe it or not, if you do, you will be encouraging her to be sneaky about peeing and she will go where you can't see her. Plus they *never* forgive you for this kind of abuse.

Keep Trying (And So Will They)

Yorkies can be challenging to potty train and even the best Yorkie can have an accident. Whether it is stress or a new person in the house, they might be excited or distracted enough to forget the potty place. In addition, once your new arrival becomes acclimated to your routine, you will know that it is not realistic to think you can watch her all the time. But they *want* to please you and with your guidance will do their best to do what's right.

Assume that all puppies must go potty after every meal, every nap, first thing in the morning, last thing at night, the minute you come home, or just before leaving. This program takes care of about 80 percent of their potties. Anticipate their routines and you will have fewer accidents.

NIGHTTIME RITUAL

There are two stages you will invariably go through when a Yorkie first arrives at your house. The first stage is when puppy sleeps all by herself, trying to get through the night on her own. The second is when she graduates, quite inevitably I assure you, to your bed. Yes, believe me, it *will* happen. If you're unwilling to share your bed with your Yorkie, you are in for troubled times ahead.

Your first night together will invariably be the most

challenging. Think of it. Your Yorkie has just been transplanted to a totally new environment with new smells, new sounds and new people. Now all of a sudden, it's nighttime and she realizes just how foreign things are and just how alone she really is at that moment.

Stage One: Getting Through the Night Alone

First, if it's a puppy, she will need to have her own area in which to spend the night. This is to prevent her from leisurely getting up during the night and peeing on the floor while you happily snore, oblivious to the havoc around you. This area must be closed off in such a way that your puppy cannot escape. I have seen people use laundry rooms and put up box fences. I have also seen baby gates work well for closing off an area. Ideally, if you use a room, it will be one with linoleum or vinyl floors (although you will be using your paper trick you learned above).

You may also elect to take the crate with the puppy into your bedroom. Maintain your usual nighttime routine and then go to sleep. If your puppy stirs during the night, for instance, whining or crying, they may need to go out and you can let her out and then she goes right back into the crate.

Have her special toy or stuffed animal for her to cuddle with in the bed (crate). I always put some dry kibble into the bed with them or next to it, so that they can nibble at night if they want to. I always want Yorkies to have food in front of them as you can never tell when they will be hungry. I've had many Yorkies that loved to crunch dry kibble at night. I could hear them crunch, crunch, crunch. I would have a bowl of dry food in the bedroom for those that slept with me so they could snack during the night.

Remember that at first she will not be able to make it through the night without a potty break. Two things may happen. You may get up during the night—say, a few hours after she goes to bed—and let her out, or you may elect to just let her use the papers. I have experience with both ways of doing this and both can work equally as well. Keep in mind that if a Yorkie becomes accustomed to being let out during the middle of the night, you could be up consistently even when she becomes older or when you are traveling.

Crating at night avoids two mishaps. First, you won't be stepping into her puddles or poo, and second, you won't accidentally step on her.

You may also use a crate as an alternative to a room, setting up the crate in a room nearby. That way, if she needs to go potty during the night, she will (hopefully) send up an alarm and you will awaken and take her out. I have also used the small "pet cab" (plastic) with bed, toys, and dry kibble for their sleeping quarters. They will need to be accustomed to it their whole life as a safe, pleasant place to rest and travel. Yorkies like its cave-like atmosphere for safety and comfort.

You may also choose to put the open crate in the laundry room and cover the floor with paper so that she can go into her crate to sleep, but can come out to potty during the night. Be sure there's no way out of the room should you choose this method.

Keep in mind, of course, that this night thing won't go smoothly at first because there's nothing she would love more than to snuggle up with mom and dad in their comforter. But this little scoundrel can't be trusted yet, as she has no qualms about where her next pee or poo happens.

Taking your puppy to bed is too dangerous during this first stage. She can become confused about where she is and fall off the bed. You might roll over on the puppy or fluff the covers and make her go flying off the bed. This is a vulnerable time for her, so keep her safe by keeping her in her own area.

When you get ready to put her to bed for the night, you can help quiet her down by taking a towel or blanket and covering their crate up. Kind of like putting a sheet over a birdcage so they will sleep. Make sure that the towel is not tight in any way that would cut off the air to the crate, but just lightly draped over so the light will be dimmed. I keep a small flashlight next to the bed so I can check on her without havintg to turn on all the lights.

Stage Two: The Bed Coup

Graduation to the bed is pretty much inevitable. Why? Let's just say that the two of you have fallen for each other so hard that you can't stand the thought of being away from each other for two minutes. Besides, it's really cute to see Yorkies making nests in your comforter and watching your baby sleep on her side.

The puppy needs to be very stable, savvy, smart and confident before you try to allow it to sleep with you. I advise waiting until puppies are older before you give them bed privileges. She needs to have an understanding of heights so she won't just randomly fly off the edge of the bed. She must know enough to move if you start to roll on her. Try lying down for a nap several times with the puppy so you can establish a pattern.

Keep her on the inside of the bed, not the edge.

When you first start the graduation to the bed, be prepared for an excited, boisterous Yorkie that is absolutely thrilled at the idea of spending the whole night with you. She may be a tough one to settle down at first, but as she gets used to the routine of bed, she will fall right into your habits. Be patient. Sometimes if you stay up later than usual, she may even stand and look at you like, okay, this is bed time, so what are you doing? Eventually, you will both settle down together happily.

LEAD & LEASH TRAINING

With smaller dogs like Yorkies, a harness puts less strain on their neck and you have an adequate amount of control over the dog. In addition, if you ever need to swoop your Yorkie into your arms for safety, you wouldn't want to end up hauling her up by the neck. Harnesses come in various colors and sizes so they can even be a fashion statement, mixing and matching with the color of the leash.

Having said that, you may want to use a collar to begin with simply because of the "head control." When you first start out leash training, you may find that your Yorkie will keep her head to the ground, taking in all the fascinating smells there.

I would only use a harness after the dog is lead trained. I have seen dogs that have been

105

taught on a harness from the start and the dog can be extremely misbehaved, standing on two back legs and pulling the owner. Using a harness from the beginning gives the dog too much control and I don't advise it.

The difference between a lead and a leash is that leashes require a collar or harness to attach it to the dog. A lead acts as a collar and leash all in one. I love leads for traveling and I personally don't like having collars on my own Yorkies, but I know that in some cases it is necessary to put ID tags on. I put these tags on their crate doors as an alternative.

What kind of leash or lead should you buy? That will depend on the size of your Yorkie. With the tinies, three pounds and under, and puppies, I use a light lead when I cannot find a harness small enough. The lead is made of lightweight nylon and at the end, loops around the dog's neck. This is a light enough weight so that the tiny's fragile neck is not endangered.

I don't usually recommend chain leashes simply because they are so heavy and not necessary for a dog the size of a Yorkie. Cloth leashes are sufficient and will give you the control you need over the dog. If you go with cloth, you probably won't need one with more than a ˘ inch width. If the lead is stiff when it's new, you can wash it or boil it in water to soften and give it more flexibility.

One note about retractable leashes. I don't like them because you cannot pull your Yorkie back; you can only let her go out further or stop her from going out further. If another dog appeared, you could not control your Yorkie with this leash. Many Yorkies have been killed by larger dogs on this retractable lead when people let their big dogs wander around (often unleashed).

How to Start

Like with anything else, your Yorkie will look speculatively at this snake-like object that has emerged from your hand. With both collar/harness and lead/leash, you need to give her some time to adjust to the idea. Don't expect to slap a collar and leash on a puppy and go for a walk without some transition time.

Start with the light lead. Show it to your dog so she can smell it and know it's not going to hurt her. At first, you can just slip it over her head and then back off again. Then praise her for her bravery. Dogs are generally leery of things coming over their heads, so it may take some time to get past this step. Just be gentle and encouraging; remember this is about trust between you and your new friend.

Eventually leave the lead on for a few minutes at a time and then take it off, praising and perhaps giving your puppy a treat. Extend this until the dog has the idea that the lead is a good thing.

The same goes for the harness and leash. Start out by letting your Yorkie drag it around the house for a while; that way she can get used to it being a part of her and not be intimidated. Make sure she doesn't get tangled up with anything and pull anything on top of her.

Obeying Lead/Leash Commands

One of the best ways to accustom your Yorkie to the leash is to bend down and pick up the leash, calling your dog to come to you. When she comes, praise her. You may encounter resistance, but keep at it. Once she has gotten used to the idea of walking around like normal on the leash, you can move the whole act outside.

Coax your Yorkie friend to follow you a little at a time until you're actually walking together. Never pull your Yorkie against her will. Wait patiently until she is ready to walk. You may bait her with cheese or a treat to reward her moving toward you. Above all, don't wear yourself or her out by trying for too long.

BASIC COMMANDS

Most people want their dog to at least be able to sit and come on command. It may also be useful for you to teach your Yorkie to stay, heel and drop things out of her mouth.

Sit

Learning to sit is the basis of all other commands and is useful for when you need to do something like put a harness on your Yorkie or put drops in its ears or brush her or whatever. Probably the best way to teach sitting is by using treats.

Stand in front of your puppy and show her a treat you are holding in your hand. Say her name and then "sit." If you then raise your treat hand over her head, she will follow it with her eyes and head and plop into a sitting position. At this point, you can praise her and reward her with the treat.

Yorkies are intelligent enough that after a few times, they will associate sitting with a treat and will sit even if they don't think you have a treat in your hand.

Come

Teaching your Yorkie to come is essential for the safety of your dog, especially when you are out in public. Start your training in this area inside the house with a leash or lead on the dog; until she is properly responsive to your command of "come," she should never be outside in an unconfined area without a leash on.

Only associate "come" with positive, rewarded behavior. If you need to discipline your Yorkie for any reason, avoid calling her to come; just go to her and handle the situation there or bring her to the situation.

With the leash in your hand, face your little character and walk backwards, telling her to come in a happy, upbeat voice. When she follows you, keep walking and encouraging her. After a little of this, bend down and hold your arms out as a welcome and give the command to come. The more praise, the more responsive your Yorkie will be. Teaching your Yorkie to come could save her life someday.

Stay

If you have the Federal Express man at the door, you don't want your Yorkie to go flying out the door onto the street (or onto the Fedex man for that matter). A good command to remedy this behavior is stay.

With your Yorkie in a sitting or standing position, raise your left hand with the palm facing her. Give the command "stay" in a firm but not overly menacing way. From there, slowly take a step backwards, maintaining eye contact and repeating "stay." Her urge will probably be to come forward to jump on you, but if that happens, just start over again.

Once you achieve a five or ten second "stay," you can praise her and reward her with a treat. You may also want to have a word that she knows is the "release" word. It can be any word you think will be easy for her to remember the sound of, preferably something simple. That way when the doorbell rings or someone knocks on the door, you give the "stay" command and your well-trained Yorkie is safely inside, out of harm's way.

If my Yorkies do run up behind me at the door, I gently use the bottom of my foot to "bat" at them, pushing them back. Soon they learn they cannot run to the front door.

Heel

Heel is a good command for a Yorkie to know because it also has a lot to do with their safety. If you are out walking together and a large dog approached unleashed, you have that much more time to react and pick up your baby if she is already at your side than if she is wandering the full length of the leash. Never mind if she charges the big dog trying to start a fight in the traditional Yorkie way! In addition to just basic safety, heel means "don't yank on your leash when we go walking."

Start with your Yorkie on a slack leash on your left side. Hold the leash with your right hand so it is across your body with your thumb looped into the leash for control. As you start walking, say her name and "heel." This is going to be a new command, so be patient and expect that she won't know what the heck you're talking about. Use your left hand to grab the leash and jerk it lightly (don't overdo this; remember, this isn't a German Shepherd).

Try again from the beginning. If she pulls or drops behind you, use your left hand and turn the opposite way. Don't worry about running into her; she must learn to stay out of your path. Doing this will teach her to be watchful of your movements. Just don't step on her!

Like any other command, heeling is about practice and repetition. The moment you get any positive response is the time to stop and praise her. Don't run this training session into the ground. Short sessions every few days keep this a positive activity where you and she have fun together instead of becoming a punishment.

Drop

Sooner or later you *will* find something in your Yorkie's mouth that you don't want there. The best thing is to address it immediately by *training* her to drop something. You may do this by giving her an object and then teaching her to release it. Get her to sit in front of you. Give her something like a rope bone that you can hold part of while she has

it in her mouth. Put your right hand under her mouth and say, "drop it." If she doesn't let it go, continue to tell her to drop it and use your other hand to gently pull the object out of her mouth. When she *does* let go, praise her generously. You can repeat this a few times in one training session.

BARKING

Yorkies have been categorized as "yappy," but there are vast differences in the amount of barking you'll get from one Yorkie to another. Dogs bark to warn other dogs off, to welcome you home, because they are enjoying playing or if they hear a strange noise. But excessive barking can be irritating and there are definitely ways of dealing effectively with your Yorkie's barking.

What you need to do as an owner is discern why your Yorkie is barking. If she is gazing at you and then barks, she probably wants to play or be loved. She might be hungry. You can deal with this special form of communication by filling your dog's need for physical exertion: walks, playing inside the house, cuddling. A tired, happy dog is not as likely to bark.

Yorkies tend to be territorial so don't be surprised if your little terror barks when someone walks by outside the house. You can prevent this by drawing the shades, but when you do, don't pet or comfort her because you will reinforce her barking habit. Yelling is another thing to avoid in a case like this, although it can be a natural reaction to barking. And again, hitting a Yorkie *never* works.

Delay the timing of the cuddling or playing so that the Yorkie does not think her barking caused you to react with playing. That would encourage more barking as well.

Water Bottle

Many people use a water bottle on their cats as a harmless way of distracting them from clawing or scratching. This can also work for Yorkies for the same reason: it startles them and becomes associated with something like barking. The instant they bark, you squirt them with water. It can be a deterrent that you may only have to use once or twice. The only disadvantage to this method is that it forces you to carry a water bottle with you around the house. For those of you who are uncomfortable with the idea of spraying your little darling in the face, you can try one of the other methods.

Citronella Collar

A recently developed product can be very effective in controlling unwanted barking. It is called a citronella collar. Using a nylon collar on which a small black box is hanging, a spray of citronella is activated by the dog's bark. This is a safe method to use even on a dog as small as a Yorkie because the citronella is non-toxic and it is about startling the dog into silence not spraying her in the face. It usually only takes a few times before she gets it. One of the most illustrative stories about how well this collar works comes from Amy Tan, a Yorkie mom herself.

A Report from the Drill Instructor of an Ex-Yappy Little Dog

I had been reading the ads for citronella collars for a long time, debating whether I should get one for Bubba and Lilliput. Their barking was not bad; at night they often were quiet for three or four hours at a stretch. But like all Yorkies, they can be fearsomely noisy when the doorbell rings, when strangers come to the door, when they are alone in hotel rooms, when neighborhood dogs bark, when the wind whistles, when the moon rises, when cat ghosts appear, and so forth.   On top of that, Bubba has been known to give people near heart attacks when he barks while secreted in his doggie bag.   We count among those nearly dying of terror around 117 airline security people, 45 shop clerks, two secret service agents.   And Lilliput, our dear little thing, thinks it's absolutely hilarious to yap non-stop whenever she sees a cat nearby.   We have many friends with cats.

Yet, in spite of the obvious need, a few factors discouraged me from trying the citronella collar:
1) Uncertainty about effectiveness
2) Size of the dogs vs. the collar
3) Uncertainty about the harmfulness of citronella to a Yorkie's respiratory system
4) Cost

Over the past few months, I had gathered enough anecdotal stories to know that the collar could work.   The biggest draw-back still seemed to be the size of the device.   Then I saw that Valley Vet catalog had the collar (made by ABS) in a size suit-able for dogs ten pounds and under.   The price was still a bit steep: around $150, plus $15 for citronella refills.   But hey, when you weigh liability suits for near-heart attacks, an invest-ment of $165 for peace and quiet is worth it.   I decided to try the collar first on Bubba, since he, at 3.4 pounds, is the more massive of my two Yorkies.

How the Sprayer Works

The device, even in the 10 pound-and-under-dog size, is bulky for a small Yorkie. It is about 2.25"H x 1.5 " W and 1.5" D. And the red snap-on collar is huge and needed to be cut down by about ten inches.   The propellant is a citronella mix—a light lemony scent—that comes in an aerosol container.   There is no finger nozzle, just the plastic tube, which is inserted into a hole in the spray device.   The device must rest against the throat of the dog and as I understand it, it is the vibration of the barking that triggers the spray.   Thus, another dog barking in the vicin-ity would not trigger the sprayer to go off.   On the other hand, if the dog is wearing another collar with metal tags and this taps against the citronella spray device, that sort of contact might cause it to go off. Once you have filled the spray device, you can test to see if it is working by blowing into the vibration sensor. A quick hiss (reminiscent of a snake's warning sound) and small burst of spray ensued: fast and startling, fragrant but not irritating.

I put the collar on Bubba and then brought out his favorite item that elicits vicious barking: a CD. (It's important not to elicit barking by giving the command "Speak" or similar cue that you have deliberately taught.) Sure enough, in seeing the flash of the CD, Bubba barked and barked and barked. Nothing happened. I then figured out that the collar was way too loose. So I adjusted it. We waved the CD again. Bark! Bark! Then "pssssstt!" Silence. Bubba ran off then stopped, looking all around. Who did that? He started licking upward as if to taste what was at the end of his snout.

We then tried a more difficult test: the vacuum cleaner. Since I have already trained him to speak on command, he also responds to "no bark," but only momentarily when he's in a terrible frenzy, as is the case when he's around a vacuum cleaner. I said "no bark" and Bubba was quiet. Then I turned on the vacuum cleaner. But after a few moments he could not resist. Bubba raced over to bite the hose. Bark! "Psssst!" Silence. He sat down, quiet. I continued to run the machine, while Bubba sat quietly and watched. This was absolutely amazing to me. Meanwhile, Lilliput was barking, still uninhibited, but after a while, perhaps because Bubba wasn't getting excited by any of this, she gave up and sat quietly as well. I praised them both: "Good, no barking!" and gave them treats. Throughout the evening, I repeated this praise. Bubba seemed especially happy that I was pleased. Lilliput looked glum.

Collar Proves to Be a Life-Saver

Shortly after this, I went to see some friends in the country. Bubba had on his collar when the friends' German Shepherd attacked him, puncturing him in the back and chest with one swift bite. Bubba squealed, which set off the sprayer, and the dog stopped the attack, dropping him. Bubba continued to scream in agony and the sprayer continued to go off. I felt terrible about that, but looking back, I think that this is what saved his life. It confused the big dog, giving us enough time to scoop Bubba up.

Because of the trauma associated with this last use of the collar, I did not use the collar for a while. Later, I talked to an animal behaviorist friend about this and he did not think Bubba would directly associate the collar with the attack, because we had done previous training with it. So we resumed, but with care and in situations that did not pose any sense of danger to Bubba.

But is it safe?

I have never seen Bubba or Lilliput act distressed by the spray's contents. That is, they do not rub their noses or eyes or even sneeze. Their reaction is mostly surprise due to the suddenness of the spray. In that respect, the device works like an instant squirt gun with a hair-trigger finger.

Recently, I decided to see if I could substitute plain water for the citronella spray. I found an Evian face mister in an aerosol can. I removed the finger nozzle and inserted the plastic tube into the device, filled it, and discovered it works with this as well. The instructions by ABS, however, do warn against using anything other than the citronella refill for purposes of the warranty. So I am not recommending you do this, except at your own risk.

In the meantime, I plan to talk to the ABS people—I have found a contact—to find out about the possibility of using water refills and reducing the size of the device even more. I feel that barking is a particularly big problem among toy breeds. And I also sense that people are reluctant to buy the citronella collars out of fear that the citronella is irritating or harmful.

While I have found nothing apparently hazardous with the collar, I usually monitor its use very carefully. The only time it is on when I am not there is when they are left alone in the hotel. And for that, I have only used it with the plain water.

"My, You Have the Quietest Yorkies I've Ever Met"

I can now say after two weeks' use that the collar does a wonderful job of inhibiting Bubba's barking in exactly those situations where I have been unsuccessful or unable to shout, "No barking!" The spray is so quick that its cause-and-effect association is obvious to the dog. We have used it in restaurants, while the dogs are going through airports in their doggie bag, when room service arrives, when guests come, when deliveries are made, etc.

I have also used the collar on Lilliput, who weighs only two pounds. She tends to bark for attention, to get cats to run, to call out to other dogs, to alert an entire floor in a hotel that she's in the vicinity and if she can't sleep, neither should they. We had not been as successful in training her to "no bark" on command. Thus, I was interested in trying the collar.

On her first time out with the collar, a dinner with friends who own two large cats, Lilliput received three sprays before she stopped barking. The rest of the evening was spent in blissful quiet. Our friends with the cats were grateful. (They had taken care of Lilliput for one week once while I was in China and said that she barked the entire time.) That evening, the cats roamed out, insouciant and unharassed. Lilliput sulked but she did not bite. Nor did she try to charge the cats to get them to run so she could chase them.

I have found that without their bark there is also no "bite," meaning, none of the aggression that usually accompanies the barking. And along with this, when one Yorkie is quiet, the other tends to follow suit.

I knew something was working when an animal behaviorist who had accompanied a friend of mine to dinner remarked at the end of the evening, "My, those are the quietest, most well-behaved Yorkies I've ever met."

Wink, wink, say no more.

117

SOCIALIZING YOUR YORKIE

First decide if you want a social dog. Show dogs must be socialized to allow other people to touch and handle them. But your pet Yorkie could be a target for theft. I hate to say this, but the truth is small dogs and cats are used by cruel people to train pit bulls and other aggressive breeds for killing. Other small dogs get sold for drug testing.

My daughter had a small dog stolen from her back yard. A well-known breeder back east had a Yorkie stolen from her patio porch and the breeder was just inside the kitchen. Believe that it can happen.

My advice is to be cautious and aware of your surroundings. As I emphasize all the time, be aware of what is around you. If you take your Yorkie for a walk and you see other people walking their dog, I would not encourage you to bring your Yorkie over to their dog to meet. A disaster takes only a few seconds to happen. Now that doesn't mean that you should never take walks with your Yorkie or go to public places with her. It just means use your head!

That said, exposing your Yorkie to a variety of environments can help with aggressive personality traits. You will be able to tell when you watch other people's Yorkies how well socialized they are. A secure, confident Yorkie is likely to greet people happily with licks and jumps, but a less secure puppy or dog may choose that moment to hide behind your legs or under the bed.

Proper socializing doesn't mean you are going to change the inherent personality traits of your Yorkie, but you will enhance her positive aspects. If she is suspect of people but not hiding between your legs, it just means she takes a little longer to trust. On the other hand, if she loves everyone who walks through the front door, she is probably going to be a "people dog" all her life.

How Do I Start Socializing?

Your socializing process is the first step in creating your role as your Yorkie's guide and mentor. Sounds silly, but it's true: your Yorkie really will look to you for the "house rules." Taking walks is a good idea because your Yorkie will always meet different people and dogs and encounter new sights, smells, and terrain.

Remember that during these stages of socialization, your dog may be afraid of things or people or she may be fiercely aggressive. My advice to you is that you don't praise fear, but you do praise normal behavior, like a puppy that can pass another dog or person without aggression or fear.

Objects

If she is afraid of something, don't shove her at the object of her fear; let her approach it and deal with it on her own terms. Remain silent if you can while she watches that soda can in the road with dark suspicion.

You can even kneel down beside the can and pick it up, showing her that it is in your hand and not causing you any harm. Don't tell her in soothing tones that it is okay; just let her see you next to the can. You may even throw the can a short distance (away from her of course) and see if her curiosity overrides her trepidation.

People

If you are introducing new people to your Yorkie, have the person kneel down so they are not towering over her. She's small enough without that! Then have your friend hold a small bit of cheese or biscuit or even put it on the ground a short distance away from her. When the ever-curious Yorkie comes exploring, your friend can slowly extend a hand to pet her under the chin or on the chest, without reaching over the dog's head, because that can be threatening. Don't expect perfection and don't react angrily if your Yorkie doesn't immediately become the perfect hostess. Just like people, it takes time to get used to new people, to trust and to make friends.

I always trust my dogs' opinions. If they don't like a person (no matter what we have tried), but like everyone else, I listen to their instincts—no matter what.

Noise

We all make noise in some way or another in the course of a day. We also experience the noise of construction work or the scream of a siren on the street. To us, this is just commonplace. To a Yorkie, especially a puppy, it can be unnerving. It's an alarm call to watch out for something dangerous or mean coming along. What you can do is to associate some realistic, normal activity that makes noise with something your Yorkie loves. For instance, if you're making a homemade meal for her, you can try mixing it in a metal pan or tapping a fork on the side of a plate. She will then know that not all noise is scary or bad. Eventually, she will become accustomed to even the most annoying noises.

RIDING IN THE CAR

Your Yorkie will most likely take her first car trip with you on the way back from the breeder's house. At that point, there isn't much of an association with cars except perhaps that when she gets in one, she goes to the vet to get shots. A change is definitely in order!

Try short trips where your Yorkie just practices getting into the carrier, being put in the car and driven around the block. Nothing bad happens there. And maybe you can even give her a treat and praise her for being such a brave girl. That's the first small step in creating the good traveler you ultimately want her to be.

Then you can try slightly longer trips, where she may be in the carrier for five to ten minutes at a time. Gradually, you can even go places that may take 30 or 40 minutes round trip (in town). In this way you are showing your Yorkie that sometimes she will go on trips and there won't be anything negative associated with them. Of course you'll obviously have trips to the vet mixed in there as well, but that's just part of the routine.

When you come back each time, praise her for being such a good girl and do something fun with her or give her a treat. After she reaches a safe age to be out in public, you may want to drive to a park and take her for a walk. This is another way of letting her know good things happen when she gets in the car.

I want to emphasize that no matter how short the trip I'm taking with my Yorkies, I *never* let them get into the car by themselves or be loose inside the vehicle. It's just plain dangerous. I'll talk in more detail about traveling with your Yorkie in chapter 9.

YORKIES AT HOME

When you are caring for a toy dog, you have to become "insightful" and start to see everything from the aspect of Murphy's Law (whatever can go wrong will go wrong). One lady tied her female Yorkie with a rope attached to her collar out on the front porch. She returned to find her strangled. This type of action may work on a large dog but not on a toy dog.

Expect your Yorkie to be capable of things you wouldn't dream of. You'll soon find out, for example, that a Yorkie can be a climber. Tenacious and armed with their claws, they can climb out of that pen or walled up area and you'll arrive home to find them running around loose. They jump, climb and pull themselves up on counters, beds, and furniture like cats. They can fit into the smallest of imaginable spaces and their curiosity can lead them to make some tight squeezes. If a Yorkie smells food on the top of a desk, she'll deduce how to get up by hook or crook. Be prepared for this endearing mixture of determination and natural wonder.

Chapter 6

Nutrition

Why worry about your Yorkie's nutrition? Your Yorkie's nutrition is central to her health, energy and overall wellbeing. She needs certain nutrients to bolster her immune system and maintain an active lifestyle. Before this, you may have believed that all you needed to do was plop down a bowl of dry dog food and go on with your life. You may have gotten this impression because no one had given you any other information. Maybe the vet you talked to didn't know any better.

The truth is you have many choices in the search for the right nutrition for your Yorkie, but not all of them are the best or even the easiest to find. Sometimes you have to take matters into your own hands for the good of your Yorkie. In this chapter, I will give you guidance about food choices for your Yorkie.

TOY DOGS & FOOD

What kind of food needs does a toy dog have that a bigger dog may not? Make sure the protein level is not too high (this will "burn out" the kidneys). I try to stay about 25% to 28% for puppies and 20% to 22% for adults. There are some dry foods that are as high as 32% and I might mix this in for a puppy diet at 10% of the regular kibble. This lets the dogs eat what they choose. Make sure food with lower levels of protein are available in this mix.

The next major concern is that the quality be first rate. I would never recommend that you buy from the grocery store shelves. The dog foods there might be fine for a larger dog, but I wouldn't trust them for a Yorkie. That was my downfall for Cari's kidney problem. She was fine until I used a "store bought" food for her. Look for the best foods in pet stores, from the vet or even via mail order.

FOOD BASICS

Food & Water Dishes

I use nothing but stainless steel bowls for both food and water. When we fix soft food like for Cari, we use small paper plates (great to throw away). Plastic dishes are porous and could harbor bacteria or rancid food products, plus puppies like to chew on plastic bowls.

Vitamins & Supplements

As a general rule for adult dogs I don't use vitamin supplements. This is if the dogs are healthy and we're having no problems. But I also feed very high quality food and they get some vegetable snacks when we make salads, or cook veggies. I feed raw vegetables twice a day every day.

Dry, Semi-Moist or Canned Food?

I feed dry food pretty much exclusively, with the only exception being Cari's Kidney Cleansing Diet, and the treats (I only feed healthy treats) that they get almost every day.

Why Buy Premium Dog Foods?

I started feeding the premium foods when I started raising Yorkies. Since they eat a smaller amount of food, they need to get the best nutrition out of each bite. Premium foods tend to have more digestible nutrients that the dog can actually use than commercial foods and we don't need fillers with these little guys.

I also tend to buy premium foods because I have had a few problems with commercial dog food. I have had some bags that were rancid (perhaps old, out in the sun, or something like that). There has been some controversy about the preservatives used. Vitamin E is my choice of preservative, and most dog foods no longer use the Ethoxyquin preservative that was used for so many years.

Another problem with commercial dry kibble is that most of it is too large for a small dog to crunch. The better quality brands will offer smaller kibble both for small dogs and puppies, as well as adult and puppy formulas.

You Recommend Any Types of Dog Food?

Over the years I've tried many different brands. I feel that dry dog food cannot stand on its own merits. That is why I use both the kibble *and* my homemade meal plan.

I have had good luck at some point or another with Wysong (our favorite one), California Natural (also a favorite), Azmira and Iams.

I've tried all of these, but right now I am feeding California Natural chicken flavor (they also have lamb and rice). I offer Wysong Anergen I mixed with the California Natural as another choice. For new puppies, I also use Science Diet Puppy Formula (canned). If these foods are not distributed in your area, you can refer to my resource section in the back of the book for contact numbers.

Snacks & Treats

I do believe wholeheartedly in personal supplements (as opposed to pills or powders). These might be made up of raw vegetables, bits of cheese, raw fruit, tiny pieces of lean steak cooked rare or medium rare (only a few bites of this last). When traveling I order steak and eggs and my Yorkies get most of the steak after I cut off all fat, gristle or bone. When I am at home, I cut the steak into tiny pieces and freeze it so I can give two or three bites at once. Go easy on the protein. I also give my Yorkies cooked eggs, cooked potato (baked or boiled) and green beans.

I only give these treats if the dog is eating normally in every other way. These treats are sporadic and spontaneous, usually while fixing meals, before or after a trip or to reward good behavior.

YORKIE PUPPIES & FOOD

Often when you get a (new) dog or puppy, they may not be eating a food that you like using. How do you make this switch without causing the dog's inner workings a bunch of grief?

Make sure you take the food that the puppy is used to home with you. Any changes need to be made gradually by offering both foods at the same time and let the puppy decide which one it wants. It takes about a week or so to make a full change. Make sure the puppy is eating the new food. Don't withdraw the old food until the puppy is well established on the new food.

How Much Food for Puppies?

As much as he/she will eat. When they turn away from the food then you'll have an idea how much to feed next time. You really have to gauge the amount and frequency of food by the puppy. Some puppies will stop eating when they are teething because their mouth hurts; some will do this after a shot. These little creatures need your constant surveillance. Remember that dry food should be in front of them at all times. Then the wet food (for puppies or tinies) offered two or three times a day until they level off and you begin to know how much they need.

When Does a Puppy Eat Adult Food?

Most dogs are full-grown at 18 to 24 months. Large dogs continue to grow for two full years while a small dog like a Yorkie is grown to their full height at 12 months but will spread out and fill out up to 18 months old. I switch from puppy to adult food at about one year.

How Often Should Your Yorkie Puppy Eat?

Depending on her age, a Yorkie puppy is a lot like a baby. They usually eat, poo, pee, play and then crash for a nap on about a four hour schedule. Even adults will eat about four times a day.

How Often Should Your Adult Yorkie Eat?

A lot depends on the size of the Yorkie. If you have a two or three pound Yorkie, you'll need to be sure they eat about every four to six hours. They are like hummingbirds with a high metabolism and a small "fuel tank." I treat small or tiny Yorkies pretty much the same as puppies, except with a lower protein in the food.

My first hard and fast rule is "Keep food available free-choice at all times." Toy dogs are not like large dogs that will eat until it is gone. If you keep dry kibble available to them, they munch along through the day because they are "nibblers."

FOOD AND HEALTH PROBLEMS

Food can be a contributing factor to water retention, obesity, enlarged heart, kidney failure, dental problems and more that I probably don't even know about. I have seen dogs scratch and chew at various parts of their bodies and all the vet could do is prescribe something topical or put them on steroids. The problem is so often internal. I have also seen people switch their dog to my homemade meal plan in coordination with a nutritionally balanced dry kibble and the turnaround is virtually miraculous.

Unfortunately the canine care population is dependent on the information that the professionals give them and the professionals and the pet industry are not going to be able to market a diet that you make at home. Therefore many of the diets you see in this book are homemade and deal directly with problems that people have had to work with. They are not commercial products.

There are commercial products that are designed to address problems or needs that your vet might recommend like Science Diet which comes in an assortment of recipes. Some are for small puppies (I use this one all the time for puppies), some for enlarged heart, and some for bladder stones. Many of the Science Diet foods are remedies for problems and not for daily use with a normal Yorkie; these are available from your vet.

Switching Food

Sometimes you will need to switch a Yorkie from a food that doesn't seem to be good enough for her or seems to be a catalyst in health problems. If the Yorkie is an established eater who is reliable on their normal intake of food, you can just switch.

If they are more finicky or don't take to the new food right away, you can mix the two together so they have both in front of them. Sometimes when I have done this the dogs will eat all around the food they don't like and spit out any that they accidentally get in their mouth. If a dog does this, I start to reevaluate the choice I have made. I believe that animals will sometimes self-regulate what they need if they have choices. I often offer several good dog foods mixed so that each has a choice and can eat differently than the others.

Food for Older or Less Active Yorkies

I really recommend the Kidney Cleansing diet (see below) that we have Cari on. Older dogs seem prone to gaining too much weight. This obesity can be very harmful and actually end their lives prematurely. As they age, they also are more susceptible to things going wrong. They have exposures to toxins and stresses and these take their toll on these little ones. Remember it is not what will go wrong but when it will go wrong. All these individuals are different and their "parts" wear out at different times (like car engines).

HOMEMADE MEALS

Why would you go through all the trouble of cooking for your Yorkie? After all, you probably work all day and barely have the energy to cook for yourself when you get home. Or you may think, I have had dogs all my life and never cooked for them and they have been just fine. Or your objection might be that it's too expensive to cook for your dog.

That is why I have set my recipes up so that you

only cook about once a week or less. You cook once, for a few hours, and then you can freeze or refrigerate the meals for that week. I keep the chicken/rice mixture in the freezer in little portion bags (I use ziplock freezer bags) and if you want to cut up the veggies to keep them readily available, store those in the fridge.

If you have been lucky enough not to suffer any health problems with the pets in your life, I will just tell you that animal foods have not escaped this age of a fast food mentality. You don't want to only eat McDonald's all the time, so why should your Yorkie?

As far as the cost is concerned, factor in all the potential short and long term problems you can have on the wrong diet (vet bills and animal suffering combined). Add in for good measure your own guilt at your pet's travails and you will agree that homemade meals combined with the proper dry kibble will benefit your wallet and your Yorkie's health more in the end.

Using Boneless, Skinless Chicken

I can't emphasize enough how important it is to use chicken without bones in it. I know that it is more expensive, but it is also less work *and* it is less dangerous. At least with boneless, skinless, you know that your Yorkie has less than a one percent chance of dying because of some bone that splinters inside their mouth, intestines or stomach.

Recently a lady who owned and bred many Yorkies decided to try raw chicken wings on the advice and encouragement of breeders on the Internet. She did it one night with all her dogs. In the morning, she woke to find her stunning 7-month-old Yorkie dead and another of her girls, four and a half months old, in severe distress.

Rushing her to the vet, x-rays revealed that her stomach was perforated with tiny splinters. Under emergency surgery, this little girl died, too. Following an autopsy on the 7-month-old, it was found that bone splinters had perforated her stomach as well. They had perforated her stomach and bowels, and peratonitis had set in and killed her.

In light of this and many other stories I have heard in my life, I can only encourage you that as you feed the chicken/rice diet, use a boneless skinless cut of chicken and to be doubly safe, also chop it up finely. You can even use a food processor to speed this process.

Kidney Cleansing Diet

I wash the chicken breasts in cold water and put them in a large pot. Put in enough water to cover them. Add a little Morton's Lite Salt to your water (excellent source of potassium). Boil chicken breasts, remove them from the pot, allow them to cool and chop them up to small bite-sized pieces. You may also use a food processor to speed this up.

Then I cook minute rice (Uncle Ben's or something similar is fine). Use the water from boiling the chicken instead of water to cook the rice.

After the rice is cooked, I mix the rice and chicken together. I have found that for about a pound or so of chicken, I use a full (medium) box of the rice. This feeds two Yorkies for approximately a week or two, depending on serving size.

Next I grate a small amount of the raw zucchini (say

a teaspoon's worth) and I chop up about the same amount of raw broccoli (florets or stem will work). The raw vegetables have the most significant source of proteins and vitamins in them; steamed broccoli is okay as well, but using raw broccoli will certainly be quicker and Yorkies love it raw. Just using broccoli as the only vegetable also works great.

I serve this vegetable mixture and the chicken/rice mixture topped with shredded cheese. For older dogs or dogs that have had attacks of pancreatitis in the past, I would eliminate the cheese. I suggest using paper plates since you can just throw them away afterwards. I usually serve this twice daily in about ¼ to ½ cup servings.

Non-Fat Diet

Boil up chicken breasts and chop them up. Take ¼ cup of the chicken to 2 cups white rice and a pinch of salt. No cheese on top of this! Mix in vegetables as usual.

Weight Gain Formula

Take ½ lb. raw ground chuck (low in fat) and mix with equal parts cooked white rice. Add ˙ cup uncooked oatmeal and one raw egg yolk. Mix well, form into balls for freezing or storage in the refrigerator, and feed 2 tablespoons each evening raw. Uncooked lean meat is more digestible, but cooking turns fat to grease.

Cari's Story

There was a turning point in my experience with Yorkies that led me to the homemade meal plan. It started when I took a trip with Cari and my other three Yorkies to Price, Utah for the Christmas holidays. I thought I took enough of their food with me, but when snowstorm after snowstorm trapped me on the other side of the mountain, I couldn't get home. Trapped there three weeks longer than I had planned, I ran out of their usual quality kibble.

I had gone to every feed store and pet store and found nothing that I felt good about for my Yorkies. In desperation, I went to the local grocery store and after spending about 45 minutes studying labels and reading every package, I picked one of the better known brands of a 'lamb and rice' kibble. I knew it needed to be small enough for the kids to chew them. That put certain limits on my choices as well as wanting to have a Vitamin E preservative as opposed to Ethoxyquin.

Skin Problems Arise

The dogs all seemed to eat it all right, so I didn't worry right away. Their stools were also all right. After about a week Cari (Ch. Lemire's What A Character) started scratching. She was incessant. When I looked at her skin, she had red splotches that I treated with *The Skin Works*. That seemed to give her some relief, but the next day she was at it again. Next, the two girls started itching as well.

I went back to the store and bought the other brand that had tempted me before. The same situation played itself out. From that time on, it was a whirlwind of trying new foods. I read the Internet list exchanges about diets and foods. It was very confusing and to make it worse, people wanted my recommendations as well.

I ordered all the best foods that had to be special ordered by phone. I can name about four off the top of my head. When someone recommended Wysong, I got the local pet store to order some. The dogs seemed to get a moderate amount of relief, but by now their coats were scratched almost down to the skin. They had ruined their topknots. But getting them comfortable was my priority.

The Peeing Problems Start

Very slowly, almost without me noticing, Cari began to urinate more frequently and seemed to be losing her housebroken qualities. Since she was also paper-trained, she would go to the white newspaper that I always leave available by the door. It seemed that she got very little warning that she needed to "go." Sometimes she would leave a trail while she was trying to get to the paper or to the door if I was trying to let her out. She was also urinating larger amounts that were almost colorless. Very disturbing!

We went to the vet as soon as we figured out that we had a problem. He needed for me to get a urine sample from her. This was not easy but soon I became very experienced at getting what I needed. She had to be "fasted" from about 9:00pm the evening before, and the sample needed to be the first specimen in the morning. This was not easy as she was not able to hold herself all night and would have accidents in her cage (apartment). I knew by her expression that she was mortified at her inability to control herself. She is so dignified and proud that this was very disturbing to her. She was 8 years old and the matron alpha bitch, aka the queen bee.

The vet said that she was in some kind of kidney failure or distress and that she needed a specialist to determine the problem. He recommended that we take her to a renowned specialist in Santa Fe, so that's what we did. He did an ultrasound of her kidneys while we watched and from there decided to do biopsies. This was very scary for both her and us. She would need to be anesthetized for this procedure and with kidneys that weren't functioning properly we were afraid of the anesthesia. This vet had a whole different way of putting her under that I'd never heard of and convinced me that it was safe for her.

Afterward, we drove home and I held her carefully in my lap, as she was very groggy. We knew it would be a week or so before we'd find out the results that this vet had faxed to our vet in Durango. Nothing showed up and we were left with only the expectation that we might not have Cari for much longer. No one seemed to know what was causing the problems and symptoms nor could they find any remedy for her.

The New Diet

About two months went by and nothing changed. I was sick about the prospect of losing my wonderful devoted companion. Then I talked to a friend of mine named Kathleen Huston. We had traveled in the motorhome (Mamu) with our dogs to Burbank to a trade show. Kathleen fell in love with Cari instantly.

She told me that she needed a special diet and that she could recover if I would follow her instructions. She told me that it would take at least five months of being on this diet in order for her kidneys to recover and return to normal. This diet was the white rice, cooked chicken, raw broccoli and zucchini topped with shredded cheese.

I began to feed all the dogs this diet and the scratching started subsiding slowly. Their systems needed to cleanse and that takes time. It seemed very compatible with the Wysong Allergen that they all have free choice. Cari can only have the rice/chicken diet; she doesn't eat any kibble (not that she doesn't sneak a bit every chance she gets!).

Health Success

Six months have passed and this week I took Cari's urine sample back in for evaluation. I couldn't believe it but the tests came back normal. I noticed that the color was the usual yellow again. She never had accidents anymore, and never had trouble holding herself through the night. We have our beloved Cari back again for many more years it seems and all because of a diet and a friend.

I've been asked to describe how I gather the urine sample. It is not exactly easy! I know that the first thing my dogs want to do in the morning is run outside and do their business. This is a routine. So I get an exercise pen set up in the back yard or on the back deck in the area that they usually go 'potty.' Then I layer several layers of the white unprinted newspaper inside

136

the exercise pen so that it is completely covered. I hand carry Cari out and put her on the paper. Then I go inside and wait with the sterile syringe in my hand ready to gather the sample. I watch out the window. You have to be patient and not in a hurry. If they can see you watching they usually will not go as they don't like to be watched.

The minute she goes potty I immediately go out and draw up the urine in the syringe and put into a plastic bag for transportation to the vet. Then I turn her loose, clean up the paper, and off to the vet I go with the sample. It's easy if you use a system like this.

Once again the Lemire household is returned to its normal chaos where Cari reigns supreme, dominating the toys, gathering the bones so she can have them all, fighting over the toys and in general taking charge just like her daddy Thadius.

WATER

There are so many opinions and controversies about water and it can be confusing to know what is the best. One thing I do know for certain is that the kind of water that not only you give to your Yorkie, but also to yourself affects the way your whole body feels. I'll outline some of the pitfalls and benefits of each type.

1. **City tap water**. This contains chlorine, fluoride and who knows what else. Chlorine is believed by many to be toxic and definitely is a carcinogen according to the professionals. The good side is that chlorine kills a majority of bacteria so that there is less chance of a contaminant bacteria getting out of control and making your dog (or you) sick.

If you are traveling in by RV, you definitely need to use chlorinated tap water for your water tank. Flush or clean your tank with an appropriate cleaning agent if the RV has been sitting for a while. Don't assume that you can just fill it if you plan on drinking any of the water (*definitely not recommended*).

Since every area has its own geological base from where the water comes, you must consider what changes might be from area to area. Mountainous areas routinely have excess minerals like arsenic, phosphorus, calcium, sulphur, and so forth. These contaminants can cause real problems when you start making changes from the water that the dog is used to at home.

2. **Bottled water—reverse osmosis**. This water can be bought at all grocery stores in gallons and 2.5 gallons; it stores very well for trips, and will cause much less gastro-intestinal disturbances than going from city to city and changing tap water. It's often called "spring" water. Make sure it is processed by "reverse osmosis." This is what I recommend that you use for your dogs' drinking water (and yours too) so that you won't be trying to clean up diarrhea at every rest stop. Even if you go visit friends or family, you will be much better off to take your own bottled water. This water doesn't have the minerals or chlorine that tap water does.

3. **Well water**. This water tastes the best to everybody from dogs to people. It doesn't have any chemical additives so it is fresh and smells wonderful. If you are used to it, no problem. But if you are used to city water, well water might have a "normal flora" of bacteria that is common to that area and the locals have no problem with, but you or your dog might not be able

to handle. This again can trigger a bout with diarrhea. Well water also has the tendency to turn rancid after a day or so in a motor home tank, so don't use it for trips. If you want to take a chance with your own body that is one thing, but for the sake of your dog, you are better off to stick to the bottled water.

4. **Distilled water**. This kind of water is boiled until it becomes steam, then condenses in tubes so that you don't get any of the minerals, chlorine, or contaminants. It is about as pure as you can get. It has fewer bacteria, depending on the handling. I use distilled for puppy formulas and sick dogs, mixing a dilution of Coat Handler sprays. You can drink it but it has a funny taste and most people don't like it. Many individuals with kidney problems only use distilled water, so this could be a factor for your dogs as well.

You can try putting two different bowls of water down for your dog, like tap water and bottled water. Watch which one they go to. They know what is best if they have choices.

EATING PROBLEMS

For the most part, Yorkies are regular eaters. They do like to nibble, though. They run around a lot during the day and burn up energy fast, so it's not a surprise to find them dropping their ball in front of the food dish and eating a few quick bites. In addition, of course, they are routine oriented and this goes for meals as well. As I said, I leave kibble free choice and add homemade meals, but you may run into a few challenges such as overeating or fussy eaters.

139

Overweight Yorkies

Hard to believe, but a Yorkie actually *can* be overweight. If you feel your dog's stomach and rib area and cannot easily feel ribs, there is a chance that your friend could have some extra padding.

I have found that Yorkies that seem to overeat and are obese are actually missing something in their diet, so they keep eating in an effort for their bodies to find the missing value. Their body keeps telling them to eat more. This is why I don't ever depend on just one diet without some variations with the treats.

I think that a lot of obesity comes from dry kibble that is loaded with too much sodium. Then there is the kind of obesity that comes from eating from Mom's plate. You'll notice that the treats that I use are not meals, not at the table and not off of my plate. I buy these treats just for their diet and they are not leftovers.

If the dog is retaining fluid, they feel spongy instead of solid. This might indicate a kidney problem. I'd put them on the Kidney Cleansing diet after having a urine sample run at the vet's.

Fussy Eaters

These dogs need to be helped through the process. I do feel that they can be taught to eat normally, but it takes strong will on the part of the owner. Remember to keep dry kibble available at all times. Also, I'd recommend getting several (maybe three) types or brands of dry kibble. Perhaps they don't like the one you offer.

I've even gotten down on the floor with them, played with them like the food was a toy. Dogs like to challenge each other for food so I try to be the one to get a game going. I spread a small amount on the floor and pick one that I toss in the air and watch it roll.

This usually gets things started. I even act like I'm eating it and then try to share it with them. The importance of this is that I don't want to feed the treat kinds of food if I can get them started eating kibble. Kibble is designed to stay in their system longer than vegetables for instance. The carbohydrates take longer to break down so they are satisfied longer.

Owners are usually to blame for a picky eater. A dog that is a favorite in the family might be a candidate to become a picky eater because it is more likely to get spoiled and fed table food as a main course. Yorkies are competitive and if there are two or more they like to eat at the same time and may become very territorial about the food. This stimulates better eating habits with the lightweights, but can go the other way and the dominant dog can starve the little one to death.

You need to observe what is going on to determine if the Yorkies eat better in competition or if they need to be fed separately. Some dogs will fight over food so care needs to be taken in determining the personalities you are dealing with.

FOODS YOU *NEVER* FEED A YORKIE

There are foods that are simply known to cause toxicity or adverse reactions in dogs. Chocolate is one of them. Chocolate has caffeine and theobromine in it, which over-stimulate a dog's nervous system and with a dog as small as a Yorkie, could be lethal. The same goes for soft drinks, coffee and tea. I avoid milk, cream, ice

141

cream. Yorkies are unable to deal digestively with dairy products with the exception of cheese, yogurt or cottage cheese, all in small amounts.

Peaches, oranges and tomatoes are okay in small amounts (like three bites) as well as bananas and avocado. I have known Yorkies that like to gnaw at an apple core a little bit after their owner is done with it. As long as you don't let it go on for too long or allow the apple core to be carried away into some private corner, I think it's probably okay.

Any food that contains or is cooked in oil or is greasy (bacon, fried chicken, fat off of steak or roast, etc.) should be considered *poison* to your Yorkie. I avoid liver, hot dogs, liverwurst or any greasy meat. No dogs can deal with cooked fat or grease safely.

Pork bones shred, crumble and splinter and can cause many terrible problems. They can get caught in the teeth or in the throat, and too much calcium can cause severe diarrhea.

So as far as bones are concerned, the only bones I've ever used with any success are large beef rib bones. These need to be boiled, stripped of *all* (and I do mean *all* since the tiniest bit of gristle left on there can cause major problems) gristle, fat, meat, or bone chips, and refrozen to harden them up again. When they look like they're 100 years old, then I let a dog have them, but only if I'm there watching and only for short periods of time (like thirty minutes). In a few days, if there are no problems, I let them chew on them again.

PANCREATITIS

Many people want to treat their toy dogs (and larger dogs too, I might add) with table scraps. It seems so harmless in the beginning. We usually leave enough on our plates or throw away as leftovers that it's a natural desire to share our tasty morsels with this charming little sweetie that doesn't eat much at all.

The problem is that it only takes one time of giving them fat, greasy bones, or spicy pizza to trigger a condition called pancreatitis. Our first case was my daughter's toy poodle. Just one spicy rib bone was all it took. Vomiting and diarrhea were the visible signs. Off to the vet. Misty was put on IV (intravenous) fluids and medication. The IV was for fluid loss and dehydration and the meds were to stop the condition. Typically this kind of trip to the vet will run you about $500 or $600.

That may sound pretty simple but it is far more complicated than that. The problem with pancreatitis is that once it is triggered, it is likely to trigger again more easily in the future. Sometimes a dog can return to a normal diet of regular dog food (not people food), but often they need to be put on a special diet designed for their condition. Occasionally the condition will continue and not respond to treatment at all. In this case, it can be fatal.

Since most of the time it is brought on by feeding table scraps or people food, it is usually preventable. I recommend only allowing the snacks and treats I have mentioned. You are *not* spoiling your Yorkie by feeding her table scraps; you are causing her problems for the future!

THE LONG HOT SUMMER

Just when I thought I'd seen it all, we watched Desi have the worst summer you could imagine. We were helping the new owners of Coat Handler move the business to Sioux Falls, SD, and I knew we'd be living in the motorhome for six to eight weeks.

Just as we were putting the final packing together, I noticed Cari (female) was just coming into heat. Oh no! Just what we didn't need. In a small space like a motorhome, there was no way I could keep the two of them more than a few feet apart. Since Desi is an experienced breeding male (Champion), his hormones were telling him "go for it!" Cari made matters worse by staying in heat for four weeks because she knows what having puppies is about and she loves being a Mom. She was watching for any opportunity to sneak a date with Desi. Since she is ten years old, there was no way I wanted her pregnant.

Poor little Desi pined his heart out for his love, Cari. When Cari had been in heat for three weeks, her daughter, Belle, came into heat. One girl usually brings others into heat. So now we were faced with a new three week heat cycle. Desi was going crazy. He whined and cried and had such a sad look in his eyes. He pawed at the cage with his front feet and tried to pee on everything in the exercise pen outside. I had two separate quarters set up inside and two separate exercise pens outside.

By the time we had been gone six weeks, Desi was an emotional wreck. What I didn't realize was it also affected him physically. As we headed for Chicago, I noticed Desi had a very swollen anal gland. I thought that after 21 years, I couldn't be surprised, but I was totally taken off guard. It came up overnight. I had bathed him the day before as we had company coming over for dinner. No problem at all and then kaboom. It looked like a red, hot walnut was sitting on the left side of his butt and it was so swollen and painful, he wouldn't let me touch his butt.

I called my vet at home. I had never had this problem before and frankly didn't have a clue what to do. He recommended that I take him to a local vet in the area and said this vet would probably want to "lance" (cut open with a scalpel to drain) the gland. I was concerned about anesthesia with a vet who didn't know me or how I approach problems like this. But my vet assured me that Desi would not have to be given anesthesia, as this was a very quick procedure that would bring relief from the pressure. A quick pain and then relief.

He was right about everything and all of us agreed that he needed antibiotic. Systemically (meaning in his bloodstream) his body was fighting the infection by walling it off and sending his white blood cells to fight the bacteria. That explained the swelling and pussy drainage. His immune system would be compromised by the infection, for sure.

I gave him antibiotics for the next 10 days by putting the pill in a piece of cheese. Desi loves cheese so he would pop it right down. After all he'd been through, he had lost weight so I was glad he would get a few extra calories. Little did I know what was coming next.

We finally got home after more than seven weeks and the first night back Desi had diarrhea. He had been running, rolling and squirreling around in the back yard when we got home so I figured it was a luscious dead worm that had upset his tummy.

I was awakened at 4:30 am by Desi making rustling noises with the paper in his cage. Each of my dogs has their own quarters for sleeping with bed, food, and water. I checked it out and he had bloody diarrhea.

I gave him 1 cc of Pepto Bismol. He immediately threw it up. That was it. I called my vets' emergency number. I told them who I was and the problem with Desi. Most of the vets know me but to be sure, I told them that this was an eight year old, five and a half pound Yorkie. I want to be sure they know how quickly they can dehydrate.

I get a call back in a few minutes from the vet on call. We arranged to meet at the clinic in half an hour. They stabilized Desi with some oral meds. When the clinic opened, they ran a blood workup and to my amazement Desi had PANCREATI-TIS. It showed plainly on his blood report. Now we all knew what we were treating. They put him on IV (intravenous) therapy to stop the dehydration. Now I'm learning new lessons about these fragile little packages.

Apparently giving Desi the pill hidden in cheese triggered pancreatitis with the high fat content of the cheese. Desi was on IVs for three days and nights. He was not allowed to go home until he could eat a little rice/chicken (no fat) dinner that we brought for him and have a fairly normal stool. Gary and I went to visit Desi twice a day. We held him and loved him to reassure him that he was going to be okay. We took his travel crate the night he was admitted and requested that he be allowed to stay in it inside the regular cage they kept him in. We also took a clean bed for the crate every day that we rubbed all over ourselves to get our smells on it. Desi would rub and roll all over the new bedding when we put it in his cage.

Well, home he came and within two days he had a loose stool again and a tummy ache. It was evening but I was afraid he might get bad in the night so I called my vets' office. One of my oldest vets was on duty. He was aware of the situation with Desi. He said he thought that with all the stress and meds and pain he'd been through, it only made sense for Desi to have a tummy ache. He suggested we go to the grocery store and buy TAGAMENT HB. He instructed that I take one pill (200 mg) and cut it into 1/10 for Desi's five pound size. I assured him that I would be very careful to cut the dose down to this tiny amount.

I hid the pill in bread this time (no more cheese for Desi). Within half an hour I could visibly see him relax and allow himself to stretch out. He had been curled up in a ball before

146

and couldn't settle down to rest. He was so relieved to have his tummy ache go away.

From there Desi has progressed very well. I learned more about Pancreatitis from this experience. Desi is now on the Kidney cleansing diet, white rice/boiled chicken breasts) and we are slowly adding a little fresh broccoli. No cheese is added for either Desi or Cari.

After about two weeks of being stabilized on this diet, I will reintroduce some dry kibble. I learned that it is better to feed more often and smaller amounts to keep from aggravating the pancreas.

When Desi goes back on dry kibble as an addition to his rice/chicken diet, I will only give him two pieces a day and work up one a day for a week or ten days. He has to move slowly into the routine diet again.

I also changed from the California Natural with 21% protein and 11% fat back to Wysong Anergen I which has a lower amount of both, having 20% protein and only 10% fat. We will see in the next couple of months if Desi can return to a semblance of a normal diet or will be too sensitive to fat and have to stay on the rice/chicken (no fat) diet.

The vet told me that he has one Yorkie patient that is triggered to life-threatening pancreatitis by a bite of potato chip. Think about how easy it is to drop a piece of a potato chip on the floor and not even know it. We can't be too careful, no matter how hard we try.

What a hard summer poor little Desi has had. He's so glad when I take him to bed for a nap while I watch TV and thank goodness he made it through his ordeal.

Chapter 7

Grooming

As with anything else in your Yorkie's life, the earlier you start with the grooming processes the better. You will notice that at first it may be a struggle—sometimes an out and out battle—but eventually you will see the dog become used to the idea of having her teeth brushed, baths, etc.

TEETH CLEANING

Teeth cleaning is essential for any dog, but for Yorkies it is especially important. As toy dogs, Yorkies have the tendency in many cases to have weaker gums and more tooth trouble. Not only can you have mild symptoms of bacteria on their teeth, like bad breath, but if you don't brush your Yorkie's teeth regularly, she can be prone to periodontal disease, which is a bacterial infection caused by plaque left on the teeth and under the gums. Signs of this can be tartar buildup and gingivitis. Poor dental health can lead to much more serious problems, like infections of the heart or kidney.

Doggy Breath

You should understand that if your dog has bad breath, she has it for the same reason you would have it: her teeth aren't being brushed. That bad breath is a sign of unhealthy stuff going on in your Yorkie's mouth. Bacteria-laden plaque collects on the teeth every time there is food in her mouth and this is what causes the bad smell. Puppies that have retained some of their puppy teeth can have a foul odor from debris that catches between the teeth. These puppy teeth usually drop out by 8 months and if not should be removed at that time.

So remember, it's never too late to start a dental hygiene program with your little squirt. Just start it the same way as you would with anything new—a little at a time.

What Does Brushing Do?

The action of brushing your Yorkie's teeth loosens the plaque built on the teeth and also can, with time, break down any tartar buildup that has already occurred. In addition, there are dog toothpastes specially formulated with an enzyme to break down the tartar and eliminate the plaque residing in the mouth.

How Much Should I Brush?

There are many different answers to this question. Some vets will advise that you brush your Yorkie's teeth every day. Others will tell you every other day or even twice every day. Of course, I like to balance that ideal with the reality of our busy lives. I have been told by several veterinary sources that brushing your Yorkie's teeth a minimum of three times a week can be very beneficial.

How Do I Brush?

The product line I have found works the best is the C.E.T., sold in veterinary offices all over the country. What is special about the C.E.T. product line is that the toothpaste has an enzymatic dentifrice that actively breaks down the tartar inside a dog's mouth. Best of all, as far as your Yorkie is concerned, it comes in four tasty flavors, which can be a big plus when you want her to sit still for a few minutes. In addition, they have a long toothbrush with two head sizes, good for getting the small and the larger teeth in Yorkies.

Start by choosing a time when you and your Yorkie are relaxed and there aren't a lot of distractions or other stresses. When you are first starting, you may want to introduce the dog first to the idea of being touched around the mouth area. Many dogs, not just Yorkies, can be wary or sensitive of their mouths and will shy away. That's why you may want to begin just by holding her and stroking the outside of her mouth with your fingers. Accustom her to lifting her upper lips to examine the teeth on a daily basis.

When she understands that you are touching her mouth and nothing bad is happening, you can try the next step. In the introductory C.E.T. dental kit, there is a finger brush that has a bristled brush. Place a small amount of the toothpaste on the bristled brush and let your Yorkie get used to you putting your finger inside her mouth. You may decide to start with a few teeth and then stop and praise her. Keep this lesson short and make it fun.

The finger brush is a good way to get the idea, but the most effective way to get rid of the plaque and tartar buildup below the gum line is going to be the brush. With a small amount of the toothpaste on the brush (I use the small end for small mouths), begin brushing in a back and forth or circular motion, similar to how you would brush. I also believe that if you put the toothpaste between the bristles instead of on top, it will be more beneficial by being closer to the teeth. Otherwise it may just fall off and roll around in the dog's mouth.

Brushing a few teeth at a time and then stopping is a good way to get going. Remember we want this to be a positive experience. You don't have to be tentative, but you also don't want to pin your Yorkie to the ground and force a foreign object into her mouth!

Over a few days or even a week, work your way around her whole mouth, paying particular attention to the rear teeth where it is most likely you would have the most plaque and tartar accumulation. Your ultimate goal can be to brush each side (or quadrant, because the mouth is essentially divided into four parts) for 30 seconds.

In general, you can concentrate on the outside of the teeth because your Yorkie's tongue should do the work on the inside. The only exception to this would be the front canines (the biggest and longest teeth furthest forward in the mouth). These need the inside brushed because the tongue doesn't do the work up there and bacteria can easily get trapped since the dog uses these most frequently for picking food up.

In addition, the motion for brushing the incisors (the teeth at the front of your Yorkie's mouth) should be slightly different. Angle the brush at about 45 degrees and start at the gum line, moving the brush up toward the top of the teeth. Because some dogs can have their incisors packed tightly together, it is important that you have a unique brushing style for these teeth.

The Path to Healthy Teeth

As long as this is a pleasant experience, your Yorkie will not resist. With patience and proceeding slowly and gently, you will turn a necessary part of taking care of your dog into a positive thing. You can even experiment with the  flavors of the toothpaste to give her a variety of tastes. Be sure and replace the toothbrush when the bristles start to bend to the outside.

Regular brushing will reduce the number of times you have to go to the vet for a professional cleaning, but will not necessarily eliminate it. It will depend to a large extent on how early you start. Nevertheless, being able to cut down on the number of times that your Yorkie goes under anesthesia is quite comforting.

Sometimes, as with an older dog, you can have the teeth professionally cleaned and be able to go from there with your home dental program. That way you are starting with a clean slate.

ABOUT YORKIE EARS

Yorkies have v-shaped ears that vary in size and shape from quite small to large and heavy. As a pet and for companion purposes, the position of the ears probably won't make a difference. They work just as well even if they "flop" or "drop."

There are several reasons why Yorkie ears may not stand up. When puppies are teething, their ears may do all sorts of things. One day up, one day down. The ear leather itself might be heavy or thick and might not allow the cartilage and muscles to hold the ears up. Keeping the hair trimmed every two weeks makes a huge difference because the weight of even a little hair can be just enough to cause the top half of the ear to drop forward.

If you want to strengthen or straighten a bent ear, you might try this. Trim the hair off the whole ear leather (at least 80 percent of the ear). Use a grocery bag (the thick brown kind) and cut a piece in the shape of the ear leather like a triangle. Make sure it doesn't go beyond the edge of the ear. In fact, cutting it a little smaller than the ear leather works well.

Take some eyelash glue (for false eyelashes) and glue the paper cut out to the inner side of the ear leather. It only has to be glued on the outside shape and a dot in the middle. This dries very quickly. Make sure each ear is shaped the same because this is how they will come out later.

153

Keep in this in place for about two or three days. By that time, you can wet the paper and the eyelash glue will loosen easily, causing little discomfort to the puppy. Pull it off gently. If you are successful, the puppy's ears will stand on their own from then on.

I feel much better about this method than taping the ears by wrapping tape around a pencil, as others have suggested. This is very hard to remove and painful for the dog as well.

EAR CLEANING

Because ears are such an open part of a Yorkie, they are also prone to problems from mites, infections or just plain dirt. The best way to keep the ears clean is to use a Q-tip. Be sure to use separate Q-tips for each ear so you don't spread any possible infections. Gently use the Q-tip and a solution like AloCetic, which you can get from your vet. This is an ear rinse that you can use once or twice weekly; it is anti-microbial and has aloe in it (but no alcohol) so it won't dry the dog's ears out. The solution acts to break up any wax or crust that may build up inside the ear.

Many times no matter how careful you are about cleaning, mites can float along and nest in Yorkie ears. Or say you have a Yorkie with "drop" ears (ears that flop over or down to the sides instead of pointing up). They are particularly susceptible to yeast infections because of the moisture that is trapped inside the ears. It is basically like a warm, moist cave and of course things start to grow. Here are a few things to watch for with Yorkie ears.

Leather Ear

This condition is notorious with Yorkie ears but it also can affect other parts of their bodies. It can be seen on the hocks, the bridge of the nose, and rump area. It looks like black tar stuck to the surface of the ear (or other area) and hair ceases to grow once it reaches a certain stage. If short hairs try to grow, they will usually come right out of the skin if you rub the black area.

What is Leather Ear?

There are many different ideas about leather ear. Some say it is a mite or insect, some say it is a fungus, some think it is contagious. I believe it is living. Whether it is an insect, parasite, yeast, mold or whatever, I do believe it can be controlled in most cases. I don't think anyone has ever proven what it is. One thing I know for sure is that if your dog has it, you want to get rid of it.

You'll know it's leather ear when the ear leathers begin to feel cold to the touch or get dark in color. Many times the Q-tip will come away with a dark film when the ears are cleaned. As the problem progresses, the hair all falls out and the ears become very sensitive to the dog. They are colder and colder to the touch and you know the dog is very uncomfortable. Many people think this is due to cold weather and call it "winter ear" as it tends to be worse in the winter.

What Causes Leather Ear?

It is important to recognize what causes leather ear or at least sets it up. Once I understood the cause, I never had a problem with it occurring spontaneously. Putting a dog "in oil" is one of the precursors to leather ear. This is because oil hinders the dog's body from maintaining its proper body temperature. This is particularly apparent in the extremities. When there is an oil spill in the ocean, one of the problems that is deadly to the animals and birds is the oil on their fur, skin or feathers. They lose their insulation properties and die of exposure (hypothermia). They can no longer control their own body temperature.

One of the next errors that set you up for the problem is shaving the ear leather. The dog needs the hair to keep the ear warm and when it is shaved the ear gets chilled and then the problem starts.

Preventing Leather Ear

I prefer to use prevention whenever possible as opposed to trying to cure a problem after it exists. So here are some tips to help prevent leather ear from getting started. As an extremity of the body, the ears are particularly sensitive to cold. This is especially true for Yorkies due to trimming the hair on the ears to get that perky little expression. But there is trimming and there is shaving. Let me explain.

I used to take a 30 or 40 blade and shave those tender little ears right to the skin. Since the majority of my dogs are all silk coated their hair grows much slower than that of the soft or woolly-coated variety. So when I shaved the ears bald, I eliminated their ability to maintain their body heat. Skin—whether it is a dog's or a human's—reacts to irritations. Cold is an irritation, therefore the Yorkie's skin begins to turn black and exudes a tarry substance as a defense. This attracts oils from shampoos and conditioners that add more layers to the black stuff.

156

So I discovered that leaving some hair on the ears was a step in the right direction. That also eliminated the problem of razor burn on the tender skin. Another irritation, of course!

Ears & Oiling

As you will learn, oil is a solvent and very drying. It also eliminates the dog's insulation and regulation of their body temperature. If show owners or handlers are "putting the dog down in oil," they not only reduce the dog's ability to stay warm on the ears, but the whole body is affected. Therefore the dog's system will protect the vital internal organs by sending the body heat to the center and reduce the circulation to the extremities.

Just trim the shape of the top half or one-third of the ear by combing the hair first to one side, trim, then to the other side and trim. Leave the surface hair in place. That is the insulation that is needed to keep the ears warm. The trimming that is done to put a shape on the ear should be done about every two weeks so that they get a little growth between trimmings. During the winter, you might allow the hair to grow longer to protect from the elements.

What About When You Have the Problem?

Now let's talk about what to do if the dog has the problem already. I have tried every cure and found some things that improve the condition but I have finally found what to me is the best treatment. I cannot call it a cure as each situation and each pet is different.

To start with, I do not believe that it is contagious because the last dog that I had come down with the condition is in close contact with my bitches that have never had the problem. He never had a problem until he was a year old and I sent him to a handler. I had never used oil on him and instructed the handler not to use any oil either. She took it upon herself to put him down in oil. Three months later when I saw him again, the skin on his back was black, he was scratching his shoulders, and he had a terrible case of leather ear. No hair grew on his ears.

It took about six weeks of using white iodine, plus Chlorhexidane, diluted 10:1 (water to Chlorhexidane), as an alternate cleaning agent. The white iodine is useful to clean inside the ear canal as well and it is more comfortable than alcohol solution. After cleaning with these agents, use Coat Handler Conditioner to swab the ear canal and coat it on the ear leather to soothe the skin and moisturize it.

When the hair begins to grow again, let it grow for a while to start holding the heat in the ears. This will help the process of recovery gain momentum.

Lessons Learned

Many years ago I used Paramite Dip which I swabbed on a Q-tip directly on the ear leather. This was on the recommendation of a veterinarian. It was strong and I think could be dangerous since dips are designed to absorb into the skin, therefore they get into the blood stream. Dips (or at least this one) cause harm during pregnancies, and in young and old animals. I have not used this method for many years, as I believe it to be too dangerous.

Now, I clean the ear *very carefully and very gently* with alcohol on a Q-tip. Use this briefly or you could break the skin (it is very tender at this point). The alcohol helps some of the black coating to break up and come off, speeding up the process of treatment. Then I use a product commonly known as Nolvasan (same as Chlorhexidane) diluted about 10:1 (water to Nolvasan). Since Nolvasan is an antiseptic, it makes me think that this problem is of a fungus type. I have also used white iodine intermittently to clean and treat ear leathers.

Then I use cotton or a Q-tip to apply the solution to both sides of the ear leather, nose or other affected areas. I do not rinse it off. I let it air dry, so this would be done after appropriate grooming. It seems to be useful to reapply every week until the problem is solved. I then apply Skin Works after the Nolvasan is dry. Within a week or so, you can see improvement and if continued treatment is followed, the symptoms seem to go away. If it should return, start treatment as soon as you see the recurrence so you can get control before the hair falls out again.

Yeast & Bacterial Infections in Ears

If you clean your Yorkie's ears out and the Q-tip comes away with dark brown or black debris, there are several possible problems. I would suspect bacterial or yeast infections, or perhaps ear mites, which I will get to after this. I have a solution that has worked fairly well for me for years. In the past I have gotten flowers of sulphur from the local drug store, but I know that now you can get a similar substance called Lotrimin from your vet which acts in the same manner.

If you have just bathed the dog, dry her ears as much as possible, then take a Q-tip and dip it in the Lotrimin,

159

lightly dusting down the ear canals. The Lotrimin also comes in a liquid or powder form. I like the powder over the liquid because you will find that when you put liquid in any dog's ears, the first thing they will do is shake it out. And it's a real mess. Besides, the whole point of the powder is to help dry moisture left in the ear and stop many bacterial, yeast and fungal problems. Depending on how bad the ears are, you can repeat this every two or three days.

If no problems exist, and you want to prevent problems, then you can use this product after each bath to keep the ears dry. Dry the ears with Q-tips after every bath. Be gentle and swab lightly with Coat Handler conditioner to sooth irritated ear canals. Dogs with down ears are much more prone to ear problems, as the ears stay moist, so if you have a Yorkie with drop ears, consistent prevention is a good idea.

Ear Mites

If you see your Yorkie flipping her head or if she scratches particularly hard at her ears, she may have ear mites. When you look in her ears and see the dark brown or black debris, that is what is left from the ear mites. Ear mites are passed between dogs or from cats to dogs. They thrive on the ear wax and debris in the ear canal. They don't bite your dog, but they can lead to an allergic reaction and severe itching and scratching.

You can use Mytox or Nolvamite (get from your vet) and the treatment usually lasts for a few weeks, which is enough to kill off the present mites and the next batch that might come along. Don't oversaturate the canals as this is disturbing to your Yorkie and may cause her enough distress to rub her ears all over the carpet and the furniture. You'll have the medication everywhere.

If the above two treatments are not effective, you can try a treatment a vet shared with me once. He said that he used Proban (cythioate 1.6 percent) which is an oral flea product, but instead of giving it orally, he would dab it lightly in the ears with a Q-tip.

If one dog has ear mites, all the dogs are probably contaminated, even if they don't show symptoms; it is highly contagious. So I usually treat all the dogs at the same time, otherwise they will pass it back and forth.

Never use these treatments on puppies under eight weeks old, pregnant or nursing bitches or older dogs without first getting your vet's approval.

TRIMMING THE EARS

I only trim ears in the V shape as an outline and only down one-third of the ear from the tip. Then I don't trim the surface hair much at all. If a dog is currently being shown, the ears can be trimmed (shape only) every couple of days. If they are home growing coat or retired, then I only trim them about every two or three weeks. It is especially important that you leave the thick hair on the back of the ear leather for warmth. If it is too long, you can comb it to one side and trim it even with the shape and then comb it to the other side and trim it to the shape.

EYE CLEANING

You will see that sometimes a brownish discharge will build up in the corners of your Yorkie's eyes. It could be that the dog has the tendency to have watery eyes or something has irritated her eyes at some point and the tearing is a natural reaction. Shampoo allergies can cause some of this buildup. Using bottled water has been shown to alleviate this problem for some dogs.

Whatever the cause of the buildup, you don't want to allow it to remain there. Not only is it somewhat irritating and unsightly, it can also harbor bacteria that can lead to eye infections.

You can take a washcloth and warm water and place it over the corner of the eye. Do one eye at a time and don't transfer the same portion of the washcloth between eyes. Letting the warmth of the washcloth lay on the buildup for 15 or 20 seconds can loosen the "crud" and make it not only much less painful to remove, but also easier.

Your Yorkie may shy away at first, but just speak gently to her and let her know what a good and brave girl she is. Hold her head firmly but not forcefully while you are wiping her eyes. Take care not to poke her in the eyes with your finger or with the washcloth. This is a quick procedure that you will want to do a few times a week, depending on the amount of buildup your Yorkie seems to have.

COAT/SKIN CARE

A Yorkie is supposed to have what is called a silky coat with no undercoat. This makes them especially sensitive to cold and also demands more attention as it can mat easily. Within Yorkie breed, there are also different kinds of coats: wooly, cottony, wiry, and combinations that a Yorkie can have. You can refer to the Resources section in this book for the outstanding coat care products from Coat Handler.

Bathing and Brushing

Welcome to the world of the long silky coat. That is what you have entered with your Yorkie. Your biggest challenge will be dealing with mats. Your essential tools are brush, comb, hair dryer, towel and the proper shampoo and conditioner. In addition, you will possibly need a detangler spray.

I start by detangling using a pin brush. This helps separate the hair to dry faster. I also use pin brushes if I want a more fluffed look when I am blow drying. At the final stage, I use a soft, fine slicker brush for tiny mats that escape the pin brush. I don't believe in brushing in between baths and I never work on a dirty coat.

I use a metal comb with fine spacing in between, especially good for working out mats and snarls. You can buy combs that have both a fine spacing and wide spacing, one on each end. A comb like this is particularly useful for finishing your brush-through and making sure you have no tangles underneath.

Unless you want to get really fancy and opt for the professional type of dog groomer's hair dryer (there are small table top models available from catalogs), a regular (human) hair dryer will be adequate. I prefer to use a hair dryer with variable speeds and temperature settings so that the air is not too hot. If your hair dryer is too hot, it can aggravate your Yorkie's skin and cause itching and discomfort, or even overheating and burn her.

As far as the towel is concerned, I keep a clean, fluffy one nearby to wrap my Yorkies in (one Yorkie per towel!) so they won't get chilled coming out of their baths. In cold weather, you can warm the towel in the dryer to help keep her warm. Use the towel to absorb excess moisture out of the coat, especially in areas that gather wetness, like the feet.

I wrap the dog in the towel and do all my brush out with her in my lap, laying on her back in the towel. I don't blow dry until the entire coat is tangle free.

Oiling

For many years, there has been a controversy raging over this subject: to oil or not to oil? For those of you not in the breeding world, when I use the term "oil," I mean to put oil on the coat to make it appear shiny.

I must admit that in the beginning of my breeding and showing career, I too, soaked my dogs in every kind of oil I could get my hands on. I tried Keri oil, mineral oil, baby oil, corn oil, almond oil, mink oil, silicone oil, and combinations of who knows what. I began to notice that I was seeing dandruff when the dog was "brought out of oil." That means "stripped" with whatever the harshest detergent available. It meant using vinegar, dish detergents (which contain alcohol detergents called ETOH) and degreasers of all kinds. Studies have shown that ETOH is absorbed into the skin and enters the blood stream as alcohol poisoning the same as wood grain alcohol poisons derelicts.

The Travails of the Skin

When I got into the cosmetic industry, I began to dig into the basics of skin, hair, and dermatology. Several things have come to light in my years of working with chemists and chemicals. I remember my astonishment when it hit me that the skin takes into the bloodstream whatever chemicals you put on it.

I watched a woman that I was traveling with put a hormone patch on her skin. Then I thought about the smoking patches and some new medication patches, and realized that the skin is an instrument of reception to the system, through the bloodstream. That explained to me, at least, why "dips" are so toxic to small or young animals. They are designed with petroleum molecules to be absorbed into the bloodstream. They overload the kidneys because some of these chemicals are not organic and put many toy dogs or old dogs into kidney failure.

Then I heard about a veterinarian who was studying the effects of oil on the ability of the animal to maintain their body temperature. They get too cold in the cold weather and too hot in the hot weather. The animals that are caught in the oil spills die of hypothermia and exposure because they cannot maintain proper body temperature. I'm sure that absorbing all that petroleum-based oil is pretty toxic to their kidneys as well.

Last but not least, all these chemicals bonding together begin to take their toll on the skin. Think of the skin like the garment when the oil stain is first seen. Every bath after leaves more and more residues (proteins, oils, conditioning chemicals, etc.). A dog's skin begins to turn black when the environment irritates it. Laying on hot surfaces and harsh chemicals are the main causes, but of course cold temperatures can trigger blackened skin as well. If the situation continues the hair begins to thin and not grow back at the usual rate. They can even begin to get pore infections, callouses and dermatitis.

Some dogs get hot spots due to the rinsing problems created by oil-based products that chemically do not rinse properly. The chemicals create heat on the skin and start an irritation, then the dog licks, scratches, or chews and bacteria take over to start an infection.

I have found that the mildest chemicals can be used when no oils or bonding type of chemical additives are used in the formulas. The milder the shampoo, the less softening effect is seen. The dog stays clean longer because they don't attract dirt like a dust rag. Then they require less bathing. The color holds up better, and they don't mat up nearly as much. Many mats are caused by chemical bonding between the hairs caused by chemical buildup sticking together (residue).

Stripping and Texture

The next thing I learned was that when you use harsh stripping detergents you pull the color out of the hair as well as the dirt. When I see a black dog that has red-tinged ends of the hair, I know they are using harsh shampoos on this dog. Most people think it is from sun exposure, but we have seen those cases turn back to a nice black color when mild shampoos are used. The first color under black is red and when you put a permanent wave or peroxide to lighten hair, red is always under the black and even blues turn to bronze when harsh chemical are used on them.

As time went on, I learned more about texture. I found out that the softer the hair, the more susceptible the hair is to damage by harsh detergents. That's right! Soft coats are more likely to get softer when harsh detergents are used. So the people who say that all soft coats have to be put in oil are setting the stage for the coat to require strippers to get the oil out and then the coats get softer and softer.

Next I found out that oil is a solvent of sorts. Ever notice how the latex rubber bands seem to dissolve when the dog is in oil? Notice how your brushes wear out quickly and the pins collapse and the pads come loose from the frame? This is because oils actually dissolve the glue and eat through the pad of the brushes.

Dryness and Static

Then I started noticing that oil has a drying effect on things. They may appear "wet," but really they are dry. Lanolin is a heavy oily molecule meant to keep sheeps' wool dry from rain and moisture. It is a moisture barrier. When you want to stop rust on your clippers and tools, you coat them with oil to keep moisture from causing the rust to form. So, again oil demonstrates its ability to stop moisture. Oil and water do not mix so oiling skin and coats actually causes dryness.

As if all that isn't enough, I then discovered that oils cause static. Yes, static is also part of the problems that you get with oils. You will have to spray more oily things on the hair to try to stop the static that is caused by the residues left on the coat.

Oil: A Permanent Resident

Next, I found out that when you use oils, lanolin, or silicones, they are not likely to come out of the hair or skin with one bathing session. I watched when an oil stain gets on my clothes. I can use shampoo directly on the stain and it won't come out. I can use laundry soap of all kinds and it still won't come out.

I also noticed that the more I washed the garment, the darker the stain became. The oil molecule was actually attracting and grabbing other molecules and bonding with them. So after many washings with many types of cleaners the stain became black. Then I would just throw the garment away.

Taking Out the Oil

Many mats are chemical mats, not actually tangles of the hair. Chemical mats (pelting) are actually chemical residues (oils, lanolin, proteins, silicones etc.) that start sticking together and forming new chemicals bonding the hairs to each other. These bonds cannot be broken by brushing, but can only be bathed out. If you try to brush them, the hair shaft itself will actually break instead.

To take a dog "out of oil" requires patience and a little extra time in the beginning. You need to bathe the dog every day or every other day for at least the first three baths. This is to get rid of the heaviest layers of chemicals. You will know if the chemical residues are still there because the dog will continue to mat very quickly (usually within two days). As the coat gets cleaner and less coated with residues it will begin to hold up longer and longer without pelting. Even soft coats can be easy to keep once they are chemically clean and the texture healed and the cuticle closed.

When people who have many dogs in oil want to convert them over, I usually recommend that they start with one or two at a time. When the first ones started are sufficiently cleaned up to hold up for a week then start a couple more. If a person with 12 dogs starts them all at once, they will pelt up all at once. Usually the person will weaken and put them back in oil.

The other trick to the process is that you should not comb the coat before the bath. With my system, you bathe out the mats (remember they are chemical mats) and always work on a clean coat.

Your equipment and tools will last much longer and be in better condition when you work on a clean coat since dirt and grime are very destructive to the tools. The dog will behave better because you won't be ripping his hair out by the roots. His skin won't have brush burns and be irritated by the ripping out of hair as well. You and the animal will be more comfortable and healthier in the long run.

Digging in the Dirt
A FEW WORDS ABOUT SILICONE

I have two viewpoints that I can speak from on the subject of using silicone products on people or animals. The first is based on my experience using it on show coats many years ago. The second is based on my personal feelings and judgment as the founder of a manufacturing company that produces products for use on animals but knows that the humans using the products are in direct contact with the same products. These opinions are my own and should be accepted from that aspect. You can form your own opinions as well.

When I used silicone sprays on show coats, my first reaction was that the immediate effect was wonderful. I got shine, manageability, and the hair seemed to have a sleek texture to it. The second time I used it on the same animal, five days later, I thought I got the same results. By the third time I used the spray on the same animal, I began to wonder what was wrong. The hair seemed brittle and a bit dry. I still didn't make the connection. I tried to use stronger detergents because the hair seemed to be oily or greasy looking. The stronger shampoos only dried the coat out more and it looked frayed.

What Are Silicone Products?

The Britannica Dictionary definition of SILICA: "A white or colorless, extremely hard, crystalline silicon dioxide, SiO_2, the principal constituent of quartz and sand."

The Britannica Dictionary defines SILICON as "a widely-distributed non-metallic element (symbol Si) prepared as a dull-brown amorphous powder, as shining metallic scales resembling graphite, or as a steel-gray crystalline mass, by heating silica with carbon in an electric furnace."

The Britannica Dictionary defines SILICONE as "any of various organosilicon compounds containing a silicon-carbon bond" their great physical, chemical, and electrical stability adapts them for many industrial uses as lubricants, greases, polishes, insulating resins, waterproofing materials, and for the making of a special type of synthetic rubber."

These definitions explained to me the greasy effects, the lubrications, and the shining aspect of silicone in hair applications.

My Own Silicone Experiences

I found that within about a month of using the spray, the Shih Tzu that I was working on was going backwards in his progress to achieve a show coat. It seemed like the silicone was next to impossible to get off the hair once it was there. Shampoos do not remove it.

Remember, anything that you put on skin (yours or your dogs) might be absorbed into the bloodstream through the skin.

Personally, I am allergic to products with silicones added. There are several face creams that I used for many years that started to cause burns and irritations on my face and hands. When I began to realize that the new trend was to put silicone (called dimethicone or trimethicone in different cases) in almost all human products for hair and skin, I started reading labels and buying products that did not contain this additive.

I have noticed that when you use products like skin creams with silicone additives, you will think your skin is smoother in the beginning but later it seems rougher and damaged. I've seen hair become so damaged and brittle that it is visibly coated and "fried" looking. In the beginning the hair too will seem moist and shiny but after repeated use it begins to break down and look frayed.

Biologically Speaking

In speaking to my chemist, I asked him if silicone biodegrades. The answer was NO. It is not organic so it cannot biodegrade. Silicone cannot be eliminated from the system through the liver or digestive system. It is very difficult to get off of surfaces because it is not water-soluble. Detergents also do not remove it, which is why it is used as a skin sealer in the products (commonly called "gloves") for protecting hands from chemicals and detergents in hospitals.

Silicone seems to interfere with other molecules that are trying to do their job, just like it breaks down rust in locks and gas bubbles in the stomach.

I wonder what effect silicone on hair that is blown around grooming shops and becomes airborne might have on groomers (pet stylists) who breathe it into their lungs, sinuses and eyes and get it on their skin repeatedly over ten or twenty years.

I have a personal belief that silicone implants cause many immune ailments in women and I just have a tiny suspicion that the silicones used in the cosmetics of today may be linked to the same problems over many years of use.

Silicones are currently being used in sprays, conditioners, antiperspirants, sun shields, suntan lotions, makeup, hand and body lotions and gas relief formulas. I would highly recommend for both you and your Yorkie's sake that you read the label before you buy!

Dandruff & Allergies

Redness, hives, chewing, scratching, sores, hot spots, and dry skin are all signs of either allergies or dandruff. Start the process of elimination by first using Odor Handler, then trying Coat Handler products instead of your regular shampoos and conditioners. This will help you determine if the problem is external. If there is no improvement, start changing food and diet.

Don't forget to change water, as this can also be a source of allergies. Dry skin and scratching are manifested in small white flakes near the root of the hair and on the skin.

Flea Dips & Other Chemicals

For those of you that don't know, a "dip" is a chemical diluted in water. The dog is then typically dipped into this mixture. Flea dips are used as a deterrent to kill fleas and by their nature they are leaving something toxic on the dog. This can then absorb into the skin. For a toy dog like a Yorkie, a flea dip is practically a death sentence. Their kidneys cannot deal with the toxicity. I am totally and unequivocally against flea dips.

So how do you deal with the invariable flea? Well, the good news is that recent advances have brought a decrease in the flea population. If you spot a flea on your Yorkie, you can bathe the dog in Coat Handler shampoo with Odor Handler mixed in. The reason that Odor Handler works in this case is that fleas have an oily layer that protects their bodies from water. Most flea shampoos have so much oil in them already that when you use them, you are just adding another layer of oil.

Odor Handler is designed to break down the oily barrier and eliminate the flea's protection, thereby eliminating the flea. If the problem is serious, you may also use Odor Handler to shampoo your carpet as it will eliminate the fleas there, too.

For prevention, I would suggest a product like Advantage or Frontline's Top Spot. These products are safe for small dogs and for puppies over 10 weeks old.

You can buy these from your vet. These are in liquid form and are absorbed into the first layer of the skin, thereby creating a sort of "trampoline" effect when fleas try to land.

Trimming Hair Around Face & Eyes

If you are going to trim hair around the eyes, take care to keep your scissors or electric trimmer pointed down or up and away from the eyes. One sudden movement, whether the dog doesn't feel like sitting still anymore or just gets spooked for whatever reason, and you could injure her severely.

Show her the scissors or whatever tool you are using from the beginning, before you do anything to her. Let her smell it, hear it run, and watch it operate from a distance. Only after she is comfortable with this foreign object will she let you get near her with it. I would rub a clipper over her body like a massage so she feels the vibration before attempting to trim with the blade. Hold the hair under her chin to stabilize her head.

You might want to trim along the bridge of the nose, following the natural curve of the face. I particularly try to keep the hair nearest the eyes trimmed so it doesn't get into their eyes. This hair also makes it difficult to completely clean the "gunk" out of their eyes. If errant hairs around the face tend to stick out in crazy directions you may elect to trim these as well. Our little Annie has a cowlick around her nose that makes her look like a punk rocker.

Topknots

You will frequently see pictures of Yorkies with the

hair on the top of their head drawn up in a bow or other hair accessory. This is called a topknot. It is not only aesthetically pleasing, but also keeps the hair out of the face and eyes of your Yorkie, which is just practical. Unless you plan to cut the top hair short, you will need to introduce the idea of topknots to your little friend as early as possible.

It seems that puppies need to learn to tolerate a rubber band very early (about four weeks old) so they will not start rubbing to get it out. Using your brush, make sure you get rid of any snarls or mats in the top hair. Then with your comb, draw the hair back from the face, holding small sections in your fingers as you gather them together. The preferred style is usually to leave a "part line" on either side of the dog's forehead area at the outside of the eyes.

I like to use the tiny latex rubber bands because I find that they hold the hair better and longer without creating mats. You may elect to put a tiny latex band in first and then follow that with a bow that also has its own tiny rubber band. I have seen people use ponytail holders as well that you can buy at the grocery store, although you end up having to wrap the excess length of the elastic around a few more times than with a rubber band.

If the dog rubs it out, just patiently comb it back into place and reset the bow. If they win this battle,

175

you'll never get them to tolerate bows or barrettes.

FOOT CARE

Just as we take care of our own feet by putting them in socks and shoes and trimming our toenails, we need to take care of our Yorkie's feet as well.

Toenails

Getting her toenails trimmed is not one of those things that will be particularly exciting for your Yorkie. But if you begin early, like from the time you first get her, she will gradually be less resistant to the idea.

One tool you can use is a hand held nail trimmer, which you can find in any pet store. This is normally a tool with handles like pliers and a round donut at the other end. When you clamp it together, a blade comes over the hole and covers it. This is how the cutting action is accomplished. Buy the size that corresponds with the small size of your Yorkie.

I don't personally like the "guillotine" type of tool. Instead I like to use nail trimming scissors because I feel I have more control over how much I cut. You can also find these in any pet store or supply catalog.

Start slowly with nothing in your hands and just touch her feet and play with them. As I have said, the more familiar your touch is to all parts of your Yorkie, the more cooperative she will be in the cases of grooming and administering of medicine.

When you finally start trimming, you may want to start with one or two toenails and see how your Yorkie takes it. Some are more reactive than others and you may have to do a few, then wait a day, then do some more, and so on. Others are very relaxed with the whole idea, especially if you are dealing with a puppy that doesn't know any better anyway.

Make sure you quit when you decide, not just because they are having a fit, but don't push the dog to the point of crying and shaking. If she is reacting very negatively, it is much better for everyone's sake to stop and try again another time. Praise her for what she has done and maybe even give her a treat. That way the experience ends on a positive note, even if you only cut one toenail.

Avoiding the Quick

The catch here is that you cut the toenails without cutting into the quick (very simply, a place where a blood vessel comes into the nail). Just as humans have a point past which cutting will hurt and bleed, so do dogs. In Yorkies, this is much harder to see since their toenails are usually black, not pink or white. I look for the point at which the nail starts to curve down toward the tip.

If you cut into the quick, your Yorkie will remember that toenail trimming is painful and it makes doing it in the future more challenging. One trick for telling where the quick is on Yorkies is to hold a flashlight up to the toenail.

Keep a container of styptic powder handy in case you *do* cut into the quick. Sprinkle this over the cut area and the bleeding will stop. This will sting a little, so don't be surprised if the dog cries. If you don't have styptic powder, flour will work just as well.

Overall, I would advise being conservative when you are first starting to trim, especially if you have not done it before. You may elect to measure your nail trimming by eighths of an inch. Better to trim more often and take a little off at a time than have a painful experience that just makes it harder to trim in the future.

Nail File

One other thing that I find works well after trimming toenails is using a nail file (emery board) or a diamond file on the dog's nails. They don't tend to be as averse to getting their nails filed as getting them cut and it can take that sharpness off the nails so you won't wince when she jumps on you. This can also be a good way to accustom a dog to having its feet touched since they can see that it doesn't hurt to have their nails filed. A standard emery board works nicely.

Timeline for Trimming

Generally, this will depend on how fast your Yorkie's toenails grow, but I find that I trim toenails about every three or four weeks. The structure of each foot affects how long the nails grow. Front feet tend to have longer nails than rear feet. One thing that can affect the length of toenails is how often your Yorkie walks on cement, asphalt or any other rough surfaces. This wears the toenails down and you may even want to do this to lengthen the time between toenail trimmings.

Actually Trimming the Toenails

There are two ways that I consider options for trimming toenails effectively and with the least trauma to the dog.

The first method involves you and another person. Pick your Yorkie up and hold her up against your chest. Let the feet dangle. The other person can then use both hands to trim the nails without having to hold on to the dog.

The trimmer should take hold of a paw, with their thumb on the pad and trim the toenails on each foot. Make sure your holder has a good grip because some Yorkies can really squirm!

The other way is for you to turn the dog upside down on the floor and hold her between your thighs on your lap (don't squeeze too hard). You can then do one paw at a time. I do this after the bath while they are wrapped in a towel; the nails are softer right after a bath so they are easier to trim and have less rough edges. Gently pull one leg out at a time and this should work nicely.

Either way, you are communicating to the dog that you are in charge without being mean or violent. Sometimes even these methods can result in a squirming, fearful dog. If that happens, figure that you are better off having the vet or the groomer do it. One thing about Yorkies is that they do have the tendency to back down to strangers when it comes to this type of thing.

In other words, since you're the mom (or dad), they may take advantage of their feeling that you don't want to hurt them and are somewhat tentative, or will give up at some point. In this case, pay the small fee for the groomer to trim the toenails in a few minutes, even though it may mean a car trip.

Of course, if you trim nails more often, they can accept it as ordinary instead of waiting until it makes their feet hurt.

Paws

The hair that grows between the pads of your Yorkie's feet and between the toenails can trap dirt, pine

needles, fleas or little mats. This can be very uncomfortable to the dog and it is easy to avoid. You want
the pads exposed so they don't stay moist. If hair
overgrows the pads, they may lose traction as well.

Trim the hair on the pads using a pair of small scissors, like you would use to cut a child's fingernails.
Hold up her foot and separate the pads with your fingers while trimming the hair as close as you can to
the pads.

Ideally, you will want to limit the hair on the top of
her foot as well, so that is doesn't hang over the toenails. You can take your same pair of scissors and
trim this hair as well, following the line of the foot.
Yorkie foot hair can be trimmed in a rounded manner
like a cat paw, so this kind of trimming is not difficult.

YORKIES AT THE GROOMER

You may elect (after hearing all of the above!) to
take your Yorkie to a professional groomer. Keep a
few things in mind. Depending on the size of your
Yorkie, you do not want to leave her for hours and
hours, waiting to be picked up or to be groomed. Arrange with the groomer ahead of time that you will
drop your dog off at a certain time and pick her up an
hour or two later. Make sure she eats a morning meal
before going; Yorkies need to eat quite a few times during the day and it is risky to have her sitting there
without food, as it is already a stressful situation for
her to be there in a strange place without you. If the
groomer is not willing to do this, find another groomer.

I cannot tell you how many times I have seen people
leave a toy dog on top of a grooming table unattended.
My first toy dog was a toy poodle. She was used to

jumping up on the dining room table and the backs of the furniture. She was being groomed one time and put on a noose. She was used to jumping off of everything so she jumped. She broke her neck and died instantly. The groomer had looked away for just a moment to get some coffee.

Larger dogs can be a tremendous hazard for a toy dog at the groomer. Caution with other dogs as well as yours is essential. Make sure that the groomer you go to understands your concerns and will use harnesses to prevent your Yorkie from moving at all and to control other dogs as well. Some groomers have certain days assigned to toy dogs for safety.

DRESSING A YORKIE

Yes, you heard me right. One of the most endearing qualities of Yorkies seems to be their love of "playing dress-up" (or *our* love of dressing them up!). Older dogs seem to enjoy a sweater the same way human seniors do; it keeps the chill off during naps. More than any other breed that I've been around, Yorkies seem to love making a fashion statement and dressing for the occasion.

I've seen Yorkies in colorful sweaters and overcoats with stripes and buttons and I have wonderful pictures of my Thadius' kids in many different "outfits." They have their Halloween costumes (witches hats and capes). I've seen tuxedos

181

(for weddings, of course) and sunglasses for summer. I've seen birthday hats, boots for rainy days, and of course an array of bows that cannot be counted.

Thadius had many, many sweaters (some his favorites) since we always lived in high altitude with snowy winters, but his very favorite outfit was his "HARLEY" leathers. I had gotten them for him in New York on a trip and when he wore them he literally strutted his stuff. They were black leather-type, with the Harley eagle, silver chains, zippers, and studs. I still have it and miss him so when I see it.

Watch the Temperature

Keep in mind what the temperature will be in relation to the weight of the clothing. If it could become warm during the day while you are gone, you should carefully decide if your Yorkie should be left alone with clothing on. If she is in a car and it is cold in the morning but might warm up later, great consideration should be given to leaving her with clothing or without.

Make sure she cannot become entangled in holes, straps or fittings.

Making Your Own Sweaters

During their growth period, Yorkie puppies change sizes very quickly. You might need a size before you can even buy one so making a homemade one can be an option (as storms can come in without notice). Use the bottom part of a sleeve of a sweatshirt or even a sweater. The stretchy wrist part goes around the neck (make sure it is not too tight), and as the sleeve gets wider it fits the body.

Cut round holes about two or three inches from the

hem (depending on the size of dog) so that the front legs can fit through them and still allow the wrist part to go up the neck comfortably. You can shape or trim the sweater so that boys can still go potty and not soil the sweater and yet it will keep them much warmer around their shoulders, neck and ribs.

This works well in the snow and wind, but a coat of some kind is better in the rain to keep them dry. Yorkies tend to lose body heat quickly because their fine silk coat cannot keep them as warm as a nice furry coat like a Pomeranian, for instance.

Buying Clothes from Catalogs

Some of the fashion articles are for fun, and some are for health and safety. And speaking of safety, it is very important that you choose your Yorkie wardrobe carefully to see that they are constructed safely. I have seen some that have loose elastic that could get caught around the neck or leg straps that could get wound around a leg or neck. Make sure you have a good fit, not tight or loose. A design can make a big difference.

If the elastic gets worn out or starts to come out of the fabric, replace the sweater right away rather than risking possible choking. The sweaters are never very expensive and it's worth it to keep your Yorkie safe. Outgrowing clothing or collars can cause restrictions on breathing and general comfort. Check to make sure the fit is right each time.

Chapter 8

Traveling With Your Yorkie

One of the best things about Yorkies is their portability. They can be easy and fun to travel with and make great travel companions, whether it's to the store or across the country. The key is to give your Yorkie time to get adjusted to the idea of travel. This starts when you get the dog.

As soon as you have your puppy's shots up to date, you can begin to introduce the idea of travelling. If you have an adult you got from a rescue or shelter, you can start as soon as she is settled into the routine. Establishing a level of confidence is vital in the beginning.

THE CARRIER

First and foremost, I want to emphasize that your Yorkies *never* go anywhere—planes, trains or automobiles—if they are not in a carrier. It is far too dangerous. Even if you just think it will be a quick trip to the store, it doesn't matter. You are protecting the life of the dog and your own life (as well as those of others) best when you keep the dog in a carrier.

Therefore, you need to introduce the dog to the idea of being in the carrier. You may have done this when you were crate training your puppy. If so, it will be that much easier to train the dog to stay in the carrier or crate for long periods of time.

For car travel, it obviously doesn't matter what size of carrier you use. You will use the size most convenient to you and most comfortable for the dog. That could be a carrier that is hard with rigid sides and a metal grate on front. It could also be the lighter and more convenient Sherpa type of carrier. I say Sherpa because I consider them the most well-made in terms of durability, but I know that there are Sherpa "clones" out there, too. I also say Sherpa, because I know that it has been approved by most airlines for pet transport. You need a carrier in which a pet can stand up and turn around in and this fits the bill for the dog's comfort and your convenience.

Other than quality, the biggest difference will be in the price. Sherpa bags will range, depending on the size and the catalog or store you check, from $60 to $100. I know that another brand that is similar, Samsonite, costs less than $50 for the smallest carrier. These are all soft-sided carriers, designed to fit under your airplane seat and to be easily handled no matter where you are.

In addition, Sherpa has recently developed a carrier on wheels, which is great for those of us who need to move through the airport fast with another carry-on bag or purse.

Louis Vuitton makes a soft-sided carrier that is available at Neiman Marcus and Louis Vuitton outlets if cost is no object. I have heard good things about this carrier—one lady said hers lasted for ten years before she had to replace the leather—and it does fit under the airplane seat as well.

Getting Used to the Carrier

As I say, your Yorkie may already have experience in this area. Or, you may have used a crate for training and want to use a soft-sided carrier for travel. In that case, you need to break her into the idea of being in the carrier for long periods of time.

The first way you can do that is to encourage her to go into her carrier, zip it up and place it by your feet, while you go and sit on your couch or in a chair. Start by doing this for 10 or 20 minutes. Then take her out and praise her and give her a treat. By doing this every so often, for varying amounts of time, while you're watching television or reading a book, you will accustom your Yorkie to the "sitting still and being quiet" part of travel.

Little by little, start picking up the carrier and moving around to different spots in the room. Move slowly so you don't frighten your Yorkie, but enough movement will get her used to the idea of stopping in many places, like in an airport, and being carried from place to place.

Too many people want to carry their Yorkie in their lap in the car. Your Yorkie may also prefer this, if you let her get used to it. After all, what dog wouldn't want to be on their mommy's lap when they are already excited about traveling (or perhaps nervous)? Don't be tempted!

Many years ago, one of my puppies was in my lap and when I opened the car door to get out, the puppy bolted into the street. The fact that this was rush hour made it nearly impossible to catch the puppy, not to mention putting myself at terrible risk.

Another time, a friend of mine had taught her Yorkie to run out the front door of her house, run to the car in the garage and jump in to the car. The tragedy occurred one time when she and the kids went flying out in a big hurry and none of them saw the dog run out with them. The Yorkie took the short cut under the car to the other side and when the daughter was seated and slammed the door, the dog was killed instantly when she tried to jump into the car.

USE YOUR CARRIER!

GETTING USED TO THE CAR

The next aspect of travel is making the transition from house to car. You may develop a word that will signal to your Yorkie that it's time for a trip. This will also tell her that she needs to get into her carrier before she goes anywhere. I use the phrase, "want to go bye-bye?" The more you teach her this, the safer she will be.

After she's in the carrier, bring it out to the car and put it where you would normally have the carrier dur-

187

ing a trip. This may be in the back seat or the front, but I also like to loop the seatbelt through the carrier handle as an extra precaution. Then you just sit there in the car. The first time you don't need to drive any- where. The point here is to get accustomed to the smells and the idea of the car. Next time, you can start the car engine so she knows what that sounds like.

After a few times, you may try a short trip, around the block, say. Keep extending the length of the trips and throw in a trip to the park for good measure, so she knows that trips in the car mean fun things for her. If every trip you take with her is to the vet, she will associate that with only negative things, like get- ting shots. So mix it up. Remember to give a treat along the way or when you return.

Dealing with Car Sickness

Yes, Yorkies can get carsick, too. If you break your Yorkie in to the idea of travelling short distances at first, instead of just springing a trip on her all at once, you will be more likely to avoid this.

However, some Yorkies have a genetic predisposition to throwing up when something they are in moves. In that case, you may want to take the pre-trip measure of giving her a little Kaopectate or Dramamine (your vet can advise you on the amount) at least 30 minutes before you plan to leave.

Your vet can also prescribe a sedative for your Yorkie. I am of the opinion that if you want to do this, be cautious about the dosage. I am more likely to ad- vocate that you break your Yorkie into the idea of trav- eling slowly enough that it becomes a positive not a negative experience. Not only can this make it a more pleasant trip, but your little friend is also less likely to get carsick.

Bring Your Own Food & Water

Whether you are traveling with a puppy or an adult, it is always a good idea to maintain consistency with food and water. This is not the time to try out that new food you have been wondering about. And a sudden change of water can inevitably create enough stress on your Yorkie's internal workings that you are likely to spend much of your time cleaning up diarrhea.

So take these words of advice: bring bottled water. You should already be using bottled water at home in their drinking dishes, so carry it with you on the road, too. Some people say you can mix the bottled water with the tap water of wherever you are, but I disagree. Consider how likely it is that chemicals foreign to your Yorkie's body as well as unknown bacteria could be floating in that water. You wouldn't want it for yourself and you don't want it for your Yorkie.

As far as food goes, I keep a little dish of kibble inside the carrier so that once the excitement of starting out wears off, they can munch and not go hungry. I also offer water every few hours as well. I don't usually keep water inside the soft-sided carrier because it is so likely to spill, but if you are using a wire or vinyl sided carrier, you will have water and food dishes that attach to the sides. Be sure your Yorkie has fresh water and food at all times.

Nutri-cal

I also bring a high calorie vitamin supplement called Nutri-cal with me whenever I travel. You can get this at a pet store or from your vet. What happens when a

Yorkie undergoes stress, such as traveling, the vet, moving, shots, having company over, or any other thing that is out of the ordinary, is that the dog gets excited and everything starts working furiously inside. Stress burns up the dog's energy level at a faster rate and can leave them with low blood sugar, which if not corrected, can be life-threatening.

All it takes is about half a teaspoon of Nutri-cal and the problem is solved before it becomes serious. Now, I say that, but I want to caution you about Nutri-cal, too. It is not a fix-all. If you are traveling with a tiny (3 pounds or less), I would not only take Nutri-cal, but also some food, perhaps some of the chicken/rice mix.

I found a clever way of transporting this food when I bought a small soft-sided cooler at the grocery store. You can fit about four or five coke cans in it, but it is the perfect size for Yorkie traveling food necessities. Fill it with some ice (I put ice cubes in plastic bags to keep the food dry or you can use the freezer "ice packs" that can be re-frozen) and put your food and bottled water inside. Zip it up and away you go.

If you travel around town with your Yorkies, keep a tube of Nutri-cal in your purse or car. You never know when you might run into unexpected problems. Once I went to town and took a Yorkie puppy with me just for the ride. There was an accident on the highway and traffic was stopped for hours. With all the cars idling and not moving, it kept getting hotter.

The young pup was getting more stressed out every moment and I didn't even have any water with me since I hadn't thought I would be gone that long. Luckily, I did have Nutri-cal and that saved the young pup from what could have been an emergency.

Potty Breaks

Think tiny bladders. I find that I end up stopping on the road for potty breaks about every hour and a half to two hours. If you have one Yorkie, put her on a lead and take her to an area that it is safe, away from other people, dogs and traffic so that she will have the privacy and peace and quiet she needs.

Be aware of what is around you! Many people who take their dogs on the road with them think nothing of letting their dogs out of the camper or the truck they are riding in. Away their dogs go with no leash. And invariably they come bounding toward other, usually smaller dogs (who *are* on leashes). This and having more than one Yorkie are two reasons I advocate using an exercise pen when you travel. And even then some people still think it is okay to walk a large dog right up on top of your Yorkie. Don't allow this to happen.

If you have more than one Yorkie, the problems of traveling are greatly compounded. It is very easy to put a lead on one dog for a potty break, but with two it becomes much more involved. If you have two at a time it is harder to pick them up and carry them to the right spot. It is more difficult to watch for big dogs that might be around who might try to attack them.

You can find exercise pens, which are nothing more than collapsible metal grating that can be set up and broken down quickly, at pet stores. Be sure you buy a high enough pen that even a large dog like a German Shepherd or a Labrador would not be able to leap over.

Bring Favorite Toys & Treats

A familiar toy can do wonders for calming a nervous first time traveler. When you get to the hotel, the little one will be so busy exploring and sniffing everything in sight, you might think she isn't interested in her toy. But believe me, it's a great thing to be able to see something she knows from home. She will eventually get into a game of it with you.

Treats are another reminder of home. Just add those to your doggie travel list and you're in good shape.

LODGING

There are quite a few motels and hotels that welcome dogs. You have a variety of books that you can find dog-friendly places to stay throughout the whole country. I have listed a few in the back of this book.

When you are traveling and you are not sure whether a hotel or motel accepts pets, you can do one of two things. You can be up front and honest about it and tell the hotel's front desk about your pet before you check in or you can try to sneak your dog in. Sneaking in will probably work in most cases, but keep in mind that if you are caught with the dog, there is the chance that you will be asked to leave. So it is up to you. Some Yorkies are so quiet that you would never know they were there. But it only takes one complaint to bring someone knocking on your door.

I consider a few things when I am looking for a hotel on the road. Is there a grassy area near the hotel or a park within walking distance? You will be making potty runs so this is important. Even an area that is dirt but cleared away of brush will work.

You may or may not elect to stay in a ground floor room. I know that if I was traveling alone, I would feel safer on an upper level room, and a ground floor room also may not be available. If you do end up in an upper level room and it has a balcony, be extremely careful with your Yorkie.

I know a lady who was traveling through Denver with her three Yorkies. She let them out on a narrow balcony to potty so she wouldn't have to go all the way down to the ground floor. There was an open grating that separated her balcony from the one next door and an open grating on the outside of the balcony. Her oldest girl, Prissy, who couldn't see very well at all, jumped through the grating to the other room's balcony and walked too far away to catch. When the lady called her, Prissy was too frightened to come and her friend that was traveling with her called the front desk to get into the next room and get the dog.

Finally, though, she knew that Prissy would come to her if she heard the sound of a zipper, which always meant to this Yorkie that she was supposed to get into her carrier. The dog came close enough to grab and a serious situation was averted. But it could have been disastrous!

My advice is that you either do not let your Yorkie out on the balcony of your room or if you do, put her on a leash first. Another alternative is that you can train your Yorkie to go potty on a pee pad or unprinted paper. That way, wherever the pee pad is, she goes safely.

Respect Other Hotel Guests

The best way for you to ensure that your Yorkies are always welcome at a hotel is for them to be good guests. That means you do your best to keep your friend quiet. One option you have for maintaining the peace is the citronella collar I talked about. If you just pop one on, not only will that dog settle down, but if you have more than one Yorkie, they all tend to catch the drift of what the collar means for them.

That also means that if there is a mess—whether it's vomiting, peeing or pooing—you clean it up. Odor Handler is great for cleaning up any mess from accidents, both stains as well as odors. Yorkies are good travelers and tend to make friends wherever they go, but no one likes to come in to clean a room and find a dog mess left behind. This will not endear you to any hotel.

If you leave your room, keep your Yorkie in her carrier or crate with a chew bone, food and water. You can't leave the dog loose in the room and take the chance that a maid will come in and leave a door open long enough for your dog to escape. Besides, she is just safer in her carrier when you are not there to supervise this new environment.

RISKS ON THE ROAD

Yes, heading out on the open road is great and I have enjoyed most of my time in Mamu (my motorhome) with the kids (usually four Yorkies). I try to balance my excitement at seeing new places with the open eyes of caution, because if I'm not looking out for my Yorkies, no one is.

Bee Stings

If you have exposure to bees with your Yorkie, you should talk to your veterinarian about a Yorkie first aid kit. Even during traveling, this could be a serious threat. Toy dogs are especially vulnerable to anaphylactic shock from bee stings. The symptoms could be slight or severe. They might range from grey or pasty colored gums (instead of a healthy colored pink), depressed attitude, red splotches on skin (check inside ears and belly area), stiffening of legs, vomiting, diarrhea, collapse, itching, swollen eye lids, hives, coughing, or any combination of the above.

Any of these symptoms could indicate that the animal is going into shock. They need immediate treatment with a steroid and/or antihistamine to counteract the shock or they could die. Minutes count when this situation happens. You only have about five to thirty minutes to reverse this situation. If you are picnicking out at a lake 60 miles from town, you could lose your toy from such an encounter, unless you carry emergency medication with you. You can refer to chapter 9 for more details about caring for bee stings.

Ticks

These little pests have varying degrees of infestation in different parts of the country. Ticks can jump down on you or your Yorkie when you are walking through a wooded forest area. They burrow their way into the skin, happily nesting there and hoping that you won't notice. That's the thing, though; you need to check for ticks on both you and your dog regularly. Of course, using a tick repellant can be effective as well.

If you do see a tick on your dog (it is a small insect that looks a little like a sliver of wood but may be different colors; or it may look like a small, round or flat marble), don't try to pull it out with your fingers.

That will only end up snapping off one end of the tick and leaving the head (the worst part) in the dog's skin. Instead, take a pair of tweezers and carefully remove the tick that way.

Also, if you coat the tick in vegetable oil, it will withdraw its head from the dog's skin because it will suffocate otherwise. I have gotten rid of ticks burrowed in the ear canal and beyond reach by using vegetable oil. Another alternative is to take a hot match (blow out the flame) and touch the body of the tick; it will withdraw its head from the skin of the dog.

Other Animals

As I mentioned above, people have this habit of letting their dogs run all over the place without leashes. Not only is it dangerous to little dogs like Yorkies, but it's also dangerous to you! I know, I have heard all the arguments about why it's okay to let a dog run around loose. I have heard the explanation from the owner that the dog would "never bite me, never attack my Yorkies," that the dog was "trained very well," etc. Despite all these seemingly logical rationalizations, dogs can and will attack, bite or otherwise harass you or your Yorkie.

I advise being aware of what is around you. Be prepared to scoop your Yorkie up if you are just walking around at a rest area. Better yet, take my advice and let the Yorkies be the last out of the vehicle—*after* you have set up the exercise pen!

Another reason the exercise pen makes sense is that Yorkies by nature are chasers. They love to chase anything that moves. You don't want your trip to end in tragedy with you calling your lost Yorkie's name after she goes chasing wildly after a squirrel or other forest animal, or worse tries to start a fight with that big dog running loose.

Mysterious Water Sources

I love the idea of a dog running and splashing through the water. But let's at least be careful of what that water source is. Is it a standing puddle? You don't want your Yorkie drinking out of this dubious water source. Is it a stream down the road from a cow pasture? Uh, I don't think that's such a good idea, do you? Clostridium is an infection that is picked up by drinking contaminated or stagnant water. Protect your Yorkie from unnecessary sickness.

Besides the obvious danger of the drinking water, a rushing river can be tempting, but think of having to leap into it to save your Yorkie that got a little too ambitious. Keep your little adventurer on a leash and this type of thing can be easily avoided.

The Beach

I haven't known a Yorkie yet that didn't love the beach and the ocean. And if you can find a deserted beach, more power to you to let that little set of four paws run like crazy. Just keep your eyes open to what's around you. And be sure that you rinse her paws off after a day at the beach. Sand can get between toenails and footpads and irritate those areas, taking all the fun out of the day. Also remember to wipe the sand out of her eyes. They love to dig and I guarantee the sand will fly when they do.

Keep Your Yorkie with You!

I can't stress this enough. For obvious reasons, I

don't leave my Yorkies in the car. The weather can either be too hot or too cold and they can suffer either way. But more importantly, they could be stolen. Cute faces in little packages, they are appealing and easy to tote.

This is why it is worth it to accustom your Yorkie to being carried with you into places. If she is used to it, she will be a good, quiet traveler. Many times, I have had a Yorkie with me inside of a restaurant and no one ever knew because she was so quiet inside her carrier, underneath the table.

As I have said, if you need to leave your Yorkie in a hotel room, always keep her in the carrier or crate that she travels in. I keep a "Do Not Disturb" sign on my door, but to be sure, I keep my Yorkies in their carriers. I also keep the carrier in a corner of the room or somewhere it's not obvious or in the way.

AIRPLANE TRAVEL

There are many advantages to Yorkies when it comes to traveling by air. First of all, Yorkies can get used to the whole idea and be quiet the whole time. They are easy to care for during the flight. In addition, Yorkies do not shed so you'll never find yourself next to a person with dog allergies complaining about your dogs.

Getting Used to Air Travel

One of the most disconcerting things for a Yorkie when she first travels by air is the noise. You can prevent this from being a problem. My suggestion is that you proceed with the idea of the carrier as I described above. But this time, place your Yorkie and her carrier on the washing machine when it is running, say, in the spin cycle. It sounds silly, but it gives your dog an idea of what the vibrations and engine noise of an airplane might be like. Of course, you don't want to let her vibrate off onto the floor! Then take her out and praise her for her bravery. Do this every so often and gradually extend the amount of time that she is on the washing machine a little more.

You can also place your Yorkie inside her carrier when you are eating dinner. Sit with the bag at your feet and eat your dinner or watch television. You may hear from the peanut gallery during this time, but don't react to her. After a little while, take the carrier to wherever your Yorkie normally goes potty with a pee pad, let her out of the carrier (you may praise her and give her a treat) and ask her to go potty on the pad. When she does go potty on the pad, give her another treat.

If you think your Yorkie doesn't need to learn to use pee pads, keep in mind that a 2 hour flight can add up to 6 hours. You need to be at the airport an hour in advance, and you may have an hour travel time in the car on the other end, too. You wouldn't hold it that long and neither should she.

Are Dogs Allowed on Airplanes?

The answer to that is a resounding "yes!" Thanks in part to the efforts of a former airline stewardess, most US airlines allow a dog on board. There are rules of course:

1) Your dog has to be less than 11 pounds;

2) Your dog has to fit in an airline approved

carrier that allows it to stand up and turn around;

3) Your carrier has to fit under the seat in front of you (remember this rule and don't let the airline assign you a bulkhead seat since it has no storage space in front of your feet);

4) Your dog has to be up to date on its vaccinations and you need a veterinary form to prove it. This is called a health certificate.

Flying To and Fro

For those of us who cannot bear to be separated from our Yorkies for two minutes, here are some things to keep in mind for different types of airline travel:

1) IN STATE: Short flights are likely to be made on small planes, so you need to check whether dogs are allowed. Some of the smaller planes have no room under the seat in front of you, and hence, dogs are not allowed. Even if Delta has taken dogs on past flights you've been on doesn't mean they take dogs on those tiny shuttles with a dozen seats. I have taken Desi on the small planes and they put him in the cargo area in the cabin where briefcases and larger pieces are stowed. I could see him from my seat and it worked out all right. Just check ahead of time since each airline is different.

2) STATE TO STATE: Be sure you have your Yorkie's health certificate for travel between states. If you are flying cross-country, and your flight requires a stop-over, make a potty break a priority. Go to the handicapped stall and spread the pee pad out. Keep your

Yorkie on a leash.

3)INTERNATIONAL: Think paperwork. Each country has its own requirements. Some like Germany and Italy insist that you use their pet travel form (same information as the U.S. form, but in their language). You can find forms at the appropriate consulates and they can be mailed or faxed to you. You can find web sites with information on each country's requirements, but contacting the consulate or embassy of the country you're visiting is safest to ensure you know what the most up-to-date requirements are.

Be prepared to go through the torture of doing this paperwork and have no one at customs ask you for it. The United States is likely to be the only customs border that will be a stickler about the paperwork. Check with the US embassy to be certain about any particular requirements at the time, such as how current the form needs to be.

In particular, you will need to make sure the rabies vaccination is current (more than 30 days but less than 12 months) in order to return to the US through customs without hassles.

"Yorkies Not Exactly Welcome"
If you're longing for the idyllic shores of Hawaii with your Yorkie at your side, think again. While Hawaii *is* part of the United States, it's an island and rabies-free; therefore it thinks about dogs a little differently. There is a lengthy quarantine of at least 30 days, too long to justify bringing your Yorkie.

Other places dogs are not welcome include:

England: there is currently a six-month quarantine.

Unless you're the queen, your Yorkies aren't coming close to the Tower of London. However, recent legislation by Prime Minister Tony Blair called the "passports for pets" plan officially comes into force in the year 2000. Blair's plan eases the restrictions on family pets, provided that the pets are carefully vaccinated and tagged with an identification microchip.

Australia
New Zealand
Sweden
Norway
Bali
China

If you are bringing a Yorkie into the US from another country you need double rabies and distemper protection since many other countries don't have rabies or distemper. The ancestry behind your new "import" does not have the genetic history of resistance to distemper, rabies and other diseases common in the US. If you plan to purchase a dog overseas, discuss this with your vet to form a plan for the wellbeing of the dog.

What About the Metal Detector?

No, you do not have to put your Yorkie through the x-ray machine at the airport. I would advocate the following advice. I calmly walk up to the security agent and tell him or her in a quiet voice that I have a live animal and how would they like me to handle it. This is not because I don't know what they will do; it is about giving them the power to decide how it is done. It is a diplomatic approach to get past a hurdle that could ostensibly send you back to the ticket counter if you fail to get through.

Normally what will happen at that point is that the agent will ask you to remove the dog from the carrier and put the carrier through on the conveyor belt. You will walk through with your Yorkie in your arms. On the other side, probably amidst copious "oohing and ahhing" about how cute she is, you will put your Yorkie back into her carrier and be on your way.

Be friendly and polite. Show the security agents the appropriate respect and you will most likely pass through the security gate without any problems.

How Do I Get My Yorkie on the Plane?

Now most airlines are dog-friendly, but not all. As far as I know, Southwest Airlines does not allow dogs and I have also heard of some smaller airlines that use tiny "puddle jumpers" that do not encourage dogs aboard either (although I imagine this is more of a space problem than anything else). Further, not all cargo space is pressurized which is a *must* for dogs to go above 10,000 feet elevation.

That being said, there are two ways you can get your Yorkie on an airplane. You can walk up to the airline counter (or arrange this in advance with your travel agent) and purchase a ticket for your dog. If you are traveling with more than one Yorkie, this will lead you to the one-dog-or-two dilemma. Since both your Yorkies are likely to be small and perhaps less than eleven pounds, you can just as easily tell them you have one. They are not likely to check.

At any rate, there is a fee of between $25 and $50 one way for your dog to travel with you in the cabin. The airline agent will then issue you a special dog ticket.

The people at the security checkpoint or at the gate that you pass through to board the plane may or may not check this ticket. Since only one animal is technically allowed "in cabin" per flight, a reservation will ensure that your Yorkie will have a secure place.

This leads me to the other way of getting your Yorkie on the plane. The size of your dog and the fact that most carriers are so innocuous looking (they look just like any other luggage you might see at the airport) can work to your advantage. I'm sure that it won't come as a surprise to you that I know people who have simply waited for an opportune moment and walked on with their Yorkie.

They didn't buy a ticket for the dog or draw any attention to the dog at the airport (for instance, they didn't take her out of her carrier). They simply walked on the airplane like there was nothing unusual. And if you think about it, there really isn't. It's not as if you are bringing a Saint Bernard on board and of course you have your airline-approved carrier.

Of course it is a risk, but more of a calculated risk than anything else. Chances are, 99 percent of the time, no one will even notice. And if they do notice, they are not likely to care. The worst that could happen is that you have to buy a ticket. So you may elect to go with this method. If another pet is reserved for the same flight, you could be forced to check the dog into cargo or leave the flight (according to FAA regulations). I prefer to have the reserved spot for my Yorkie.

In-Flight Comfort

Some people recommend not feeding your Yorkie anything to eat or drink at least two hours before the flight. This is probably not a good idea for Yorkies, but it's really not a good idea at all for tiny Yorkies. They could easily become hypoglycemic or dehydrated after many hours in flight.

Your alternative is to give them food and water during the flight and have them trained to go potty on command on pee pads. If they are adept at this potty on command system, then you should have no problem taking them to the airplane bathroom and letting them use a pee pad on the ground.

Some people also carry a syringe to drop water directly into their Yorkie's mouth if they cannot place a bowl of water inside their carrier without it spilling.

Plane Sickness

Dogs just like people can get sick at inconvenient times. Be prepared in advance for the possibility that your Yorkie might suffer from a bout of vomiting or diarrhea. Bring the wet naps (like the ones used on babies), pee pads, and plastic bags.

You may also want to carry a travel-sized bottle of Kaopectate. Know the dosage in advance as each Yorkie's needs differ by their size.

If you find that your Yorkie is either unable to settle down and sleep or be calm on a plane (or car), or if your dog tends to get sick as a rule, you can ask your vet for ace promazine. This is a tranquilizer that acts to calm the dog emotionally, making her groggy most likely for the duration of the trip. I would use this as a last resort, when you have a dog that just can't travel well, no matter how much you try.

TRAVEL ACCESSORIES

Depending on what your mode of transportation is, there are all kinds of interesting and helpful travel accessories that you can get for your Yorkie. Since water is a constant demand, you may buy collapsible nylon bowls that are very small. However, anything that is small will work. In times of desperation, I have even used a bottle cap.

One of the nice things about the Sherpa company is that they sell a travel pouch that you can attach to the side of the Sherpa bag and carry lots of Yorkie essentials in. For instance, I tuck my bottle of de-ionized water in there for easy access during the flight. I also keep a small bag of kibble as well as any cleaning up type of necessities.

If I ship a dog by cargo, I put ice cubes into the water tray instead of water. It slows down the spillage and makes the water available longer.

Boat Safety

For those of you brave enough to bring your Yorkie boating with you, I suggest a doggie life vest. It was a bit of a challenge to locate a vest that will fit a Yorkie, but I found one made by Safegard in Upco's catalog. Made of water repellant nylon over permafoam, it has adjustable nylon webbing and safety buckles. More importantly, there is a web handle for easy rescue. The smallest one I found was for dogs between two and ten pounds.

BOARDING

Sometimes it's not practical to take your Yorkie with you when you travel. During those times, you want to make sure that she receives the best quality care you can find. I'm not crazy at all about the idea of boarding my Yorkies in a kennel. I prefer to find someone who can take care of my dogs in my home, someone who can recognize if there is something medically amiss with my Yorkie and take the necessary action.

If finding such a person is not possible, your next alternative becomes boarding in a kennel. I would advise that you board with your veterinarian because at least that is someone who you can trust to watch out for your Yorkie's health. But be sure that there will be someone supervising the dog 24 hours a day, seven days a week. Remember it wouldn't take long for a sick Yorkie to slip past the medical point of no return. There isn't much grey area to work with.

In general, you want to be sure that the kennel is well-maintained, has high enough enclosures to prevent escape, and has separate dividers between the animals to prevent any accidental rendezvous. Yorkies are ingenious escape artists when they want to be. All it takes is a small gap or hole between pens and you have a fugitive. Request a review of the quarters your dog will be in.

I bring my dog's own food and bottled water as well as bedding. There's no reason for my Yorkie to suffer not only the separation from me, but also go through the torture of diarrhea because of a change in food or water. Given the fact that you will likely board at your vet, vaccinations such as bordatella should be commonplace. Plan in advance to have your dog current on her own vaccinations. In addition, immunizations should be up to date for all the animals that stay there.

Travel List

- ✈ Bottled water (de-ionized)
- ✈ Food (dry kibble & chicken sticks)
- ✈ Dishes that hang on exercise pens
- ✈ Exercise pens
- ✈ Clips to secure pens
- ✈ Shade tarp
- ✈ Bedding (two sets for travel crates plus some for exercise pens)
- ✈ Paper towels & Kleenex
- ✈ Small & large plastic bags for cleanup
- ✈ Large strips of white unprinted newspaper folded
- ✈ Small congoleum patch
- ✈ Lead/Leash, collar/harness
- ✈ Brushes, combs, rubber bands, bows, scissors, Q-tips, nail scissors
- ✈ Shampoo, conditioner, detangler
- ✈ Indoor/outdoor carpet or substitute for covering pavement
- ✈ Coat Handler Sunscreen Spray
- ✈ Coat or Sweater
- ✈ Towels
- ✈ Blow Dryer
- ✈ Medicines for you and dogs (Pepto Bismo—Tagament HB 200mg, Kaopectate are also fine—shock treatment for bee stings, disinfectant, wound dressing, etc.)
- ✈ Kaolyte
- ✈ Thermometer (rectal)
- ✈ Syringes (3 and 12 cc)
- ✈ Spray bottle (for cooling Yorkies down if it's hot)
- ✈ Skin Works
- ✈ Odor Handler
- ✈ Nutri-cal
- ✈ Gun and/or Mace (if you are driving in remote areas)

Chapter 9

Emergency Situations & Treatments

Prevention is the best treatment of all for most emergencies, but some accidents can't be avoided. In these cases, a calm head and a prepared household (or car) can make the difference in caring for your Yorkie.

I always emphasize that you carry your own Yorkie first aid kit (outlined at the end of this chapter for your convenience). Keep it up to date and throw away old medications so that if an emergency situation arises, you will always know that, short of a miracle, you have done all that you can for your friend.

BEE STINGS

A bee sting can happen accidentally or can be the result of an overly curious Yorkie. The symptoms for bee stings will vary in severity. Check your Yorkie's gums. Are they grey or pasty colored (instead of a healthy colored pink)? What is the dog behaving like? Is she moping around? What about her skin or body? Red splotches on skin (check inside ears and belly area) or stiffening of her legs can indicate that she has been stung. You may also see vomiting, diarrhea, collapse, itching, swollen eyelids, hives, coughing, or any combination of the above.

Any of these symptoms could indicate that the animal is going into shock. Administer a steroid such as dexamethasone or an antihistamine to counteract the shock immediately; time is precious in this kind of situation. If you are within 20 minutes of a vet, you may go there, but if not, her life is in *your* hands. This is another imperative reason that you should carry a Yorkie first aid kit with you at all times.

BLEEDING

If your Yorkie has been bitten by another animal or has been cut or punctured, no matter how it happened, use a towel when you approach her to protect yourself. You want to immobilize her. If this is a puncture or surface type of wound, you can apply pressure with a clean towel. If the wound is something different, like a torn toenail, pressure will not help.

Above everything else, the first thing you go for in a bleeding situation is hydrogen peroxide. There are a number of reasons for this. Pouring hydrogen peroxide over a wound creates oxygen in the area and battles anaerobic bacteria that are responsible for infections like gangrene, tetanus or blood poisoning. In addition, hydrogen peroxide will aid the blood clotting process and slow the bleeding. So don't worry about *how* you get it on your dog, just get it on her wound!

Depending on the severity and depth of the wound, either place a call to your vet or simply get in the car and drive. Sometimes the minutes it takes to call can spell the difference between life and death and if you show up with a wounded animal, they will not turn you away.

BROKEN OR FRACTURED BONES

Jumping is something that Yorkies do all the time, probably without thinking about it. But the landing part can be hazardous. Many times Yorkies have misjudged the distance to the ground or someone has turned their back for a second and the dog goes flying down to the floor because she thinks it isn't far. Obviously the best medicine here is prevention, but you cannot always control your little risk taker.

If you see your Yorkie jump down and then start limping or start crying, the first thing you can do is to immobilize the dog. Come up under her body and tuck her close to your body, so that if she has in fact broken or fractured one of her legs, she won't be able to put any weight on it. Be aware that if she has hurt herself, she may snap at you, so you would be wise to approach her with a towel or blanket. In this way, you will effectively take her legs away from her and prevent further injury to the area. Don't attempt to set or splint the area by yourself. There could be bone splinters inside that you cannot see and you will also make it worse trying to fool with it unaided. In addition, it is possible that she could go into shock from the injury, so it's important to keep her warm.

Be on the phone to the vet while you are holding the dog to control her movements. Watch her gums for shock (color would be grey or bluish).

If you are alone and need to get to the vet, my advice is that you call a taxi. The reasoning here is that the best thing you can do for your Yorkie at this point is to make sure she doesn't run around or put any weight on the break or fracture. If you have a neighbor or a friend you can flag down, you hold the dog in a towel and the friend can drive. In this case, I make an exception to the carrier rule for going in the car. Why? Because if you put her in a carrier and she tries to keep her balance or tries to get up, she may aggravate her injury.

CHOKING

How often does your Yorkie grab a few kibbles of food from the dish and run off to eat in privacy? Well, sometimes that can be dangerous. If you find your Yorkie making strange, forward motions with her head, she could be in the process of choking. This happens when the dog tries to swallow something too big or tries to eat too fast and doesn't chew the food enough. The particles get stuck in their throat and as with humans, you don't have much time. Take your finger (this will only work if you don't have long fingernails) and open the dog's mouth. Push your finger down her throat and with any luck you will free the obstruction to continue on its way down.

I have also gently pressed down on a dog's ribs and the thing jammed in her throat has popped out that way as well (a bit like the Heimlick maneuver).

CONSTIPATION OR BLOATING

You will know that your Yorkie is bloated or constipated because she may pace and act agitated, plus she will not have had regular bowel movements. Constipation can occur from exactly that: *not* having regular potty times. For instance, if you leave the house and are gone longer than you expect, that means your dog will have to wait longer to relieve herself. This in itself can create an unhappy, constipated dog.

The fastest way to ease her constipation is to give her a teaspoon of some type of vegetable oil. This will help lubricate her insides and you should see results fairly quickly. You can also try a baby enema using warm water. You can find these at the grocery store. Just follow the instructions on the package.

Constipation can be prevented by using the rice/chicken diet from chapter 6. Also make sure that your Yorkie has plenty of water to keep things moving along inside normally.

DEHYDRATION

Animals as well as people can dehydrate for a number of reasons. Some of the causes could be stress, illness, trauma, travel, too long between meals, etc.

Puppies can easily become dehydrated from the start because they are born dehydrated (bony and frail looking). Only after they nurse do they become plump and filled out. That is because colostrum (the first milk from nursing mothers) is about 90% electrolytes. Usually within 24 hours the milk will change to the whiter, real milk that contains more solids.

Many times puppies get dehydrated due to a bacterial cause and they actually have diarrhea and lose fluids through loose stools. Look for yellow spots on the bedding. Healthy puppy stools are very well formed and do not leave stains on the bedding.

Puppies that are dehydrated look dull and their coats are fluffed out instead of slicked tight on the body. Black coats take on a bronzy caste and they look rough. The pups get what I call "chicken necks," which is thin necks and shoulders. Dehydrated puppies do not object when you lay them on their backs. They are listless and do not have good reflexes. Often they are cool to the touch because their body temperature is going down.

If a bacterial problem exists, your vet will probably put the dog on an antibiotic, usually a liquid. Two hours after the antibiotic is given, I recommend giving some acidophilus or bacillus that can be purchased from a health food store. This replaces the stomach's bacterial flora that has been killed by the antibiotic. If you do not replace the bacteria, the puppy will not be able to digest her food. That could cause more problems with growth and weight gain.

If a puppy will not accept fluids or voluntarily drink or eat, you will have to intervene at this point to save her. I take Morton's Lite Salt which is 50% potassium and dextrose (available from drug stores in liquid or powder form) and mix it with distilled water. If you do *not* have dextrose in powder or liquid form, you can use karo syrup, honey, or any kind of jelly, like grape or strawberry (these alternatives are listed in order of use preference).

If you have Pedialyte or Kaolyte, you can use this solely and not have to mix anything.

214

My formula for a dehydrated puppy is at least 24 hours on Pedialyte (the rehydration formula) or home-made electrolytes given by tube feeding 1 cc per ounce of puppy weight every two hours. That would mean a 4 oz. puppy would get 4 ccs of electrolytes six times a day or 24 cc in 24 hours. You can see just how much fluid a puppy goes through once you calculate it out.

If the puppy stabilizes, meaning starts to hydrate, looking shinier and plumper as well as gaining strength, then I would mix 1/4 milk formula with ∫ of your electrolytes. Once they have hydrated for 24 hours, I give the combination of electrolytes with formula every four hours at 1 cc per ounce of body weight. If they continue to do well and gain weight, the third day I go to the mixture of half electrolytes and half formula. I stay on this mixture until they are eating on their own.

The key to getting dehydration under control is the potassium deficiency that causes the appetite to become depressed (therefore they stop eating) and eventually heart failure. If you just use honey or karo syrup mixed in water, you are missing the key ingredient that could possibly reverse the process. Morton's Lite Salt contains 50% Potassium Chloride and is useful whenever dehydration is a problem.

My friend Kris can recount her episode with Candy when he began to vomit for no reason. She called me for advice. It was late at night and a weekend so getting her veterinarian would have been difficult. She was hoping I could help get the problem under control before it became an emergency.

I told her to stop giving him anything by mouth for at least four to six hours. Every time he would vomit she would give him more to eat or drink and that would start the whole cycle again. Here's the solution. Get some lean ground chuck at the grocery store. Boil it in water until the meat is cooked. Add some Morton's lite salt and strain the meat out of the broth. Throw the meat away, let it cool and offer the broth to the dog.

Start with one tiny teaspoon. If he keeps that down for a half an hour, give him another. Wait for about an hour. If he holds that down for an hour, try a tablespoon. Wait another hour. You could then mix a little bit of electrolytes (Pedialyte) with the broth.

She couldn't believe how Candy responded. This was an adult dog of 4.5 pounds that could have dehydrated rapidly if not gotten under control. The key is to quit giving them anything for many hours until the gut calms down. Then start out slowly to introduce fluids again. The Tagament HB 200mg (1/10 of a tablet) would have helped in this case, too.

HYPOGLYCEMIA

Hypoglycemia is the reverse of diabetes. It occurs when sugar or dextrose levels become very high. The sugar is processed very quickly and "burned up" by the body, leaving the insulin level high and causing insulin shock. When a diet of proteins and carbohydrates are fed, they are converted into sugar more slowly and the insulin is used at the same rate as the digestion occurs. That's the basic biological explanation.

This can happen if a dog becomes stressed, if a dog is very small, if a dog is injured or if a new routine is introduced, like traveling, new people, etc.

What you will see in terms of symptoms in your Yorkie is listlessness, a "limp" body attitude, inability to walk, loose stools. This is because the dog has literally run out of fuel. There is nothing left in the body to process and to use as energy to live.

In my experience, the best thing that you can do in a situation like this, and it is a frequent possibility with very tiny Yorkies especially, is to *feed the Yorkie!* Try getting her to eat something like plain steamed or cooked rice; this is something that will not be hard on her system. Also boil some chicken and feed the dog that, if she will take it. Chicken sticks are a fast, easy pick-me-up. If she refuses to eat food at all, you might have to force Nutri-cal to offset the high level of insulin. Once this balance is reached, they will usually start eating food again.

Posie was five months old and only weighed 18 ounces. That in itself was a problem and a miracle at the same time. The breeder that this lady, Dianne, had gotten her from had given very strict instructions about feeding her: what as well as when. She was supposed to eat a type of canned food that was mostly water and had a protein level of only eight percent. This was to be given twice a day and in between, about three or four times a day, Posie was to have a boost with Nutri-stat (like Nutri-cal).

When Dianne called me panicked, Posie had become limp the previous afternoon and was unable to walk. After a visit to their regular vet, the diagnosis was that Posie had gas in her stomach and the vet instructed Dianne to withhold food and water since Posie had some loose stools.

Posie's condition did not improve overnight and Dianne took her to an emergency vet. Posie's glucose level tested at 25 at that point. This vet gave her electrolytes with dextrose, and had a stint (the feed mechanism for a catheter, like they use for IVs) in her leg, preparing to give her fluids internally. After this, they proposed to leave Posie alone for several hours, although their prognosis was that she didn't have more than two hours to live.

Dianne took Posie from them, unwilling to leave her there unsupervised. When they got home, Posie was so weak she couldn't even raise her head up. Her eyes just stared ahead. It was then that she called me.

I asked Dianne if she had any baby food and luckily she had chicken sticks. I told her to get one and mash it up fine and see if Posie would eat it. Posie ate the whole thing! Now that I knew that Posie wouldn't die while we were on the phone, I explained to Dianne that Posie was starving to death! She needed real food!

Then the cooking got started. Dianne cooked white rice and mixed that with a mashed up chicken stick. Posie ate every morsel. Then she boiled chicken breasts, added the Morton's Lite Salt and the vegetables and Posie was on her way to recovery, eating that mixture every three hours until Posie refused it after which she went to six hour intervals and finally twice a day.

Why had this happened? Products like Nutri-stat and Nutrical are loaded with calories and dextrose. They should be used occasionally for traveling, baths on young puppies or for injuries. They can stimulate appetite in puppies or adults who have gone too long without eating. When Dianne was giving that tiny amount of canned food that contained a few carbs a little protein and mostly water, it didn't use up much of Posie's insulin. But when she regularly pumped Posie with Nutri-stat, her insulin level would pop up, but then she would have what essentially was a sugar crash. Up and down, up and down...naturally giving the supplement would pull her out of the insulin weakness, but would just set her up for the next attack.

Toy dogs are a blur of activity while they are awake and then run out of gas and are ready for a nap. Most Yorkies are nibblers and that's why it's always good to have kibble free choice for in between meal energy boosts.

Within about five days, Posie was eating regularly, was full of energy and learning to bark her little head off. Dianne has added the dry kibble so Posie can chew and crunch like the big kids. Now Dianne only gives the Nutri-stat supplement for stress times.

IMPACTED STOOLS

Yorkies have a lot of hair—everywhere! This includes around the rear end and what can happen is that the dog tries to go potty and the poo essentially gets trapped in the hair surrounding the anus, creating a sort of cap. Typically, the dog may "scoot" or wipe her butt on the floor to try to wipe herself off. She will also try to keep pottying if you do not take care of her problem right away. This can lead to a blistered, puffy rectum as things literally back up.

Not having regular bowel movements can cause the bacteria count in the bowels to become too high. In turn, this leads to diarrhea, colitis, and vomiting. The condition is potentially life-threatening.

Your most immediate concern is to free the obstruction. This means either combing out the hair away from the rectum or, in the worst case, cutting the obstruction free so that the rectal area is clear.

Next you want to ease the dog's discomfort. Take some Skin Works and gently apply it to her blistered areas. This is a biodegradable, anti-bacterial formula that contains no aloe, no steroids, is non-greasy and will stop the pain and inflammation; you can apply this liberally several times a day until the redness is gone and it's truly one of the kindest things you can do for your Yorkie.

A trip to the vet may also be warranted, as he may want to put your dog on an antibiotic to control the abnormally high bacteria count in the intestinal tract. This can cause diarrhea so the antibiotic might be necessary to get the balance back.

LOST YORKIE

Nothing is more nerve wracking or heartbreaking than a Yorkie (or any pet) being lost. Whether it happened by an open door, forgetfulness, or a hole in the fence, nothing makes up for the anguish that you go through. So be prepared ahead of time with your thinking and plan of action, so that if that awful moment ever arrives, you will already have thought things through.

Another thing. Keep in mind the characteristics of your Yorkie as well as the breed in general. Yorkies like to burrow and make nests. Are there areas where your Yorkie might have hidden out, waiting for you to come and get her? Things like that are important to remember when trying to figure out the possible behavior of the dog.

They are curious and have no fear. I lost a Yorkie I had named Goody in a turntable corner cupboard when she stepped inside to check out all the interesting smells. After two hours of searching the entire neighborhood, I found her with a confused look on her face like, what took you so long?

Post Fliers

Fliers are a good way to alert people in your neighborhood about a lost Yorkie. Put them up on telephone poles, trees, bulletin boards at grocery stores, post offices, and other nearby public areas, like parks or schools. Be sure to include your phone number, details about the dog, and a reward announcement. My advice is that you don't specify the exact amount of the reward, only that it is large. When someone calls you with information about your dog or says they have your dog, get an address and a phone number and get over there asap! Do not be tricked into sending money to people who claim they have seen your flier and might have your dog.

Your flier should be something like this: LOST, Female Yorkshire Terrier, CALL 555-1234, LARGE REWARD!

Humane Societies, Shelters & Animal Control

You should visit every animal agency in your city and county. Why do you need to go in instead of just calling? Many times there are people who only answer phones and are not actually aware of new animals that have come in. With any luck, a person finding your dog will bring the dog to one of the agencies and it will be logged in there.

In addition, when you have lost a dog, you should go in person to log your dog in so that if someone calls and wants to know if anyone is looking for a missing animal, the two will connect. It may help to bring in a current photograph of your Yorkie if you have one to leave with the agency for identification purposes.

Local Area

Start your search by walking around your neighborhood, calling or whistling to your Yorkie. Keep your voice calm and upbeat; remember your dog knows if you are angry or upset and may not come to you if you sound like that.

Extend your search area to surrounding neighborhoods. You can go door to door and find out if anyone has seen anything. You may drop fliers at each house in the areas nearest to you. Driving in your car with the windows down may expedite your search as well.

Yorkie Rescues & Clubs

Check with rescues and clubs in your areas. Some people, not knowing what else to do with a lost animal, turn to a breed-specific group or individual. Your Yorkie might be there, among other Yorkies, waiting for you to pick her up.

On December 19, I got a call from Dianne and she was panicking because Prissy was lost. What??? Yes, when Dianne went to pick her up from the airport she went to the cargo delivery and waited for her plane to arrive. Now, here she was! Dianne opened the crate door because she was so excited to see her. Dianne was wearing a fur coat with long sleeves and when she reached into the crate to get Prissy, poof, she was out of there in a flash. Out the cargo entrance door and across the parking lot. Dianne screamed and ran after her, but was no match for Prissy.

It was snowing lightly and there was a layer of about an inch that was sticking to the ground. It was about 6:00 pm, so it was dark already. Although she chased Prissy up onto the main street and down the street, Dianne fell on the pavement and could only watch devastated and heartsick as Prissy disappeared into the night.

To Prissy, there was a big bear that had gotten her at the airport and was reaching right into her crate to grab her after her scary flight. Prissy ran for her life.

Now, Dianne knew that it was a life and death situation to find and catch Prissy. When she called me, I gave her the names of a couple of Yorkie friends in the area that might help. They looked everywhere, but no Prissy. After several hours of exhausted and sometimes tearful searching, they had to give up for the night.

The next day, in the morning, Dianne went immediately to the local Humane Society and registered Prissy as missing. Again, Dianne and the group of friends searched all around the airport. You can only imagine the vehicle traffic, never mind if she got out on the runway!

No luck. No Prissy. The fact that she had a red sweater on made it possible to see her with the snow as a background. So they could only hope that someone would see her and take her in.

That evening, Dianne's daughter took a call from a lady who said she had a Yorkie. The daughter identified many things about the dog, but the caller was still reluctant to give her any information about whether it was her Prissy.

Later in the evening, the lady called back and spoke to Dianne. After Dianne explained what had happened to Prissy, the lady told her, "I have your dog." She worked near the airport and had walked out of the building for her lunch break. There was Prissy. She was curled up close to the building for shelter. The lady walked up to her real slow and coaxed her to let her pick her up. She was cold and starving. The lady took her into the building and kept her under her desk. Then she took little Prissy home that night, about 70 miles away in a little town.

When Dianne got the call, she drove out immediately to the lady's house and gave her a reward in cash. The lady admitted that she was tempted to keep her because she was so darling. Finally, though, she checked with the Humane Society, knew that someone would be looking for her and followed up with the phone call.

We all smile in relief every time we think of the time that Prissy went home the long way. Prissy is now 11 years old and settled into the family routine with two other Yorkies. She finally quit running.

POISONING

The key sign that your Yorkie has something poisonous inside her is that she can still pull herself up on her front legs, but she has lost the ability to control her rear end. In most cases, the dog tries to stand on all fours but the back of her collapses. This includes accidental ingestion of medication as well as something obvious like licking at a puddle of antifreeze.

In many cases, you can use hydrogen peroxide (one teaspoon per ten pounds of body weight) to induce vomiting and remove the toxin from the dog. However, there are cases where you do *not* want to force the dog to vomit because certain things will burn going down *and* coming back up, causing more trauma than necessary.

Medications can be necessary but need to be given respect and care. I'll never forget the horrible incident that occurred when I put a pill meant for me in my pants pocket and went to work. I intended to take it as soon as I got to work. I also took a four-month old Yorkie puppy named Gypsy as my companion at work.

I got down on the floor to play with her and didn't see the pill fall out of my pocket, but she did. She acted fine for a while but when her urine turned orange I knew what she had done. I called the vet. He confirmed that it was too late, she died within 6 hours. Her lungs filled with foam and she suffocated-an allergic reaction. I was devastated for days. I felt so responsible. One little mistake and she was gone.

I have learned since that tylenol can cause liver damage. Aspirin should be "baby aspirin" (1/8 of the normal dose) and then only one quarter (1/4) of a pill for a toy dog. Never give aspirin if bleeding might be an issue since it thins the blood and reduce clotting.

Most medications for humans are dosed at toxic levels for toy dogs. Some medications that are pediatric formulas can be helpful when used by veterinarian specifications. Benadryl might be needed for allergic symptoms, but only the tiniest bit. I once had a puppy have a severe allergic reaction to a vaccination and started coughing along with huge hives all over her body. Her eyelids swelled and I knew she was going into a respiratory problem. I had given her some dexamethasone (steroid) at the first sign of a reaction (itching) but she continued to worsen. I thought of the benadryl for antihistamine therapy so I cut the smallest pill in half and then shaved off barely enough to be seen (probably 1/15 of the pill) and it did the trick. It also made her very groggy and uncoordinated. I had to keep her confined in an exercise pen for the night.

UNCONSCIOUSNESS

As a jumper, your Yorkie is liable to be knocked unconscious or at the very least have the wind knocked out of her from falling, hitting her head, or an object falling on top of her. The worst case scenario in this type of situation is swelling in the brain or broken bones.

If she is able to swallow on her own, you can break up a dexamethasone into quarters. Put your finger in something like butter and poke the pill down her throat. Dexamethasone is a steroid and is best in cases where there is no surgery necessary, no cut or wound. In a case like the unconsciousness, the steroid will stop the body from sending fluid into the brain and creating cranial pressure. You must have the dexamethasone in your house at the time because quick action is required.

Don't use the dexamethasone for cuts and wounds or

anything that will need to be operated on because it will actually retard the healing process. Use this only with the advice of your vet.

VOMITING

Some cardinal rules apply to caring for a Yorkie that is vomiting. Number one, withdraw all food and water immediately. Usually, the process of vomiting starts a spastic reaction of the muscles in the stomach, and if you put more food or water (or if the dog does) into the stomach, it just triggers another spasm and she will vomit again. As this cycle continues, she will lose more and more body fluids and actually dehydrate faster.

This is one of the reasons the veterinarian want to keep the dog when they start vomiting so that they can control the intake of anything by mouth. Most owners want to fill that stomach as fast as the dog will allow.

Your dog should not be given anything by mouth for six to twelve hours after vomiting to make sure that she is stabilized. If she has diarrhea as well, she may need IV (intravenous) fluids or sub-Q (sub-cutaneous) fluids to rehydrate her, without putting anything into her stomachs to trigger the vomiting again.

You want to try to determine the cause of the vomiting as quickly as possible. It might be Giardia, Parvo, Corona, poisoning, swallowing something, pancreatitis, over eating, motion sickness, shock, or several other things. If you don't know the cause, you should contact your veterinarian immediately and discuss your plan of action. They can run blood tests to help zero in on the cause.

I might try to handle diarrhea by myself if I think I can get it under control but when I see vomiting, that's the time when I get the veterinarian involved. Vomiting is life-threatening, as it relates to dehydration.

YORKIE FIRST AID KIT

Ace Promazine
Baby Chicken sticks
Batril (antibiotic)
Benadryl syrup (for coughing & allergies)
Betadine
Chicken/rice mixture
Cipro
Clavamox
Dexamethasone (steroid & anti-shock)
Electrolytes (either Pedialyte or Kaolyte, which comes in packets)
Hydrogen Peroxide
Lactated Ringers (solutions of rehydrating fluids with 5% dextrose & electrolytes)
Nutri-cal (for emergency stress situations)
Odor Handler
Panalog
Skin Works (for hot spots & other skin ailments)
Valium

3 cc syringes
12 cc syringes
Culture sticks
Heating pad
Needles
Pill cutter
Q-tips
Small bottle with eyedropper
Thermometer (rectal)

Chapter 10

Health Care & Diseases

ALLERGIES

Did you know that your Yorkie can suffer from allergic reactions in much the same way that you do? Allergy symptoms don't usually present themselves until the puppy is between 9 and 12 months old. You will invariably see many of the same signs as in yourself: skin welts, hive-like swellings, sneezing, itching, wheezing, runny eyes, and possibly vomiting or diarrhea.

The Solution

In a coated dog like the Yorkie, the scratching associated with allergies makes the dog very uncomfortable. Therefore, you will be acting in her best interest to take her to the vet and have a simple blood test performed. The dog's allergic reaction to certain allergens will be ranked on a scale from zero to six, with six being the highest reaction level.

The treatment for allergies will consist of hypo-sensitization by injection—a mixture of what your Yorkie is specifically allergic to. I feel this is the best treatment because it doesn't have any of the side effects of cortisone or antihistamine type drugs, and only occasionally has side effects at all. The process of hyposensitization takes care of about 60 to 80 percent of dogs with allergies; the treatment does take time, however, sometimes as long as four to nine months.

After this treatment ends, a maintenance injection may be given once a month for life.

COLLAPSED TRACHEA

There are several ways a Yorkie can get this problem. One is genetically, which means a weak trachea. Another way is that the trachea can be damaged by a lead or collar around the neck and a dog that pulls really hard against it. Lastly it can be caused by the intubation tube used by vets to give the gas anesthetic during dental cleaning or other prcedures.

I know a lady who had a little male Yorkie that this happened to. He was only two years old and perfectly healthy. She took him in to have his teeth cleaned and for days after that he coughed and could barely breathe. The vet generally says that this is normal for one or two days because there is sometimes a reaction to the tube being in the throat, but it should go away quickly.

In this case, the little Yorkie got better for a time and only had an occasional coughing spell; then he got a red throat and went down fast—and all this happened within four to six months. Once the trachea is damaged it remains weakened and the dog sounds like he is strangling and gasping for air at the same time. Basically they are coughing and trying to open the airway back up and that is why the sound is so weird. What has taken place is that the trachea has actually collapsed— sometimes in more than one place—and that is what makes the dog gasp for air.

There is currently a new surgery being experimented with that replaces the rings of the traches with artificial ones. Ask your vet for more information.

The Solution

When I have a Yorkie intubated for dental or OFAs I always request a medication called Torbugesic (5mg— cut into 1/4 tablet per dose). This medication stops the reflex that starts the coughing.

I have it on hand for the wakeup time. One or two coughs are about all I let go. If the coughing continues after that, administer the pill as I indicated. It usually only takes one dose to stop the spasms and no more coughing. This medication may make her a little groggy, so keep her resting in a crate or exercise pen for a couple of hours after the medication. If you let the coughing get into a full episode for a couple of hours, it takes more to stop it and the medication is not as effective.

In some cases, the vet gives Torbugesic as a pre-anesthetic "cocktail" to reduce the swelling and potential coughing that can follow a dental procedure.

COPROPHAGY

This is a fancy name for stool eating. If you have

ever experienced this, you will know not only how nasty it is, but also how frustrating it really is, too. It usually starts when the dogs are puppies and we think of it as a "bad habit."

My own experiments have held up to the following theory. If your dog has the habit of eating stools, or recycling food, as some people call it, I believe it is a problem with the food, not the dog.

The Solution

Many people are familiar with the controversy over Ethoxyquin, a preservative used to keep dog food from spoiling. I have found that if you try other dog foods and go to a dog food that is preserved with Vitamin E, the situation improves. It takes about a week for the full change to take effect. Lowering the protein level down to about 20 percent can also make your situation better.

According to my theory, the Ethoxyquin is so efficient at preserving the food that the dog's digestive system cannot even break it down. Therefore the food is "unprocessed" when it leaves the dog's body and has "food appeal" to the dog. Since Vitamin E breaks down better and is digested, the stool no longer has the attraction as food and they leave it alone. Keep this in balance, however; if the level of Vitamin E gets too high, the same problem occurs.

You can at least try it. Also, I use about two or three different "toy kibble" so that they have variety and I am not totally relying on one dog food to fit all needs.

Another thing that I recommend is to give a few small pieces of banana a week. The potassium in a banana can help reduce the dog's craving for what she sees in the stools or loses in loose stools—again, the undigested food material.

I had a situation with a Yorkie that I treated for eating stools as if she had a stomach infection. She was vomiting and I was concerned about the amount of e-coli bacteria in her upper gastro-intestinal tract. I was particularly nervous since she was vomiting to the point of foam. I started her out with one-half to one cc of Pepto Bismol, then I gave her dexamethasone to prevent shock and to calm her stomach down.

After she had kept that down for at least 30 minutes, then I wanted to kill the bacteria so I gave her batril (enrofloxycin, a cousin of a human antibiotic), a highly effective, broad spectrum drug. The combination of these seemed to calm her down considerably and she didn't have any more symptoms after that (except for being exhausted from all the vomiting!). After several hours of not vomiting, I gave her a tiny amount of the chicken/rice mixture. By the next day she was normal.

GENETICS & GENETIC DISEASE

Pull a few hairs out of your Yorkie's tail. At the bottom of a few of those hairs you will find a tiny root. That root contains about 40,000 cells. Within each of those cells is about six feet of genetic material called DNA—your Yorkie's entire genome. The information encoded inside the nucleus of each cell is a unique blueprint of what makes up your Yorkie.

This blueprint is absolutely specific to your particular animal and this identifies your dog unconditionally among all other living things, animals and vegetables.

From research into the genetics of animals, veterinary medicine has been able to identify diseases that have genetic causes.

Liver Shunt

Known formally as Portosystemic Shunt, liver shunt has run rampant through Yorkie bloodlines for years. Why? Because breeders do not breed it out or stop breeding it in. Therefore it is a reality that we have to deal with, and it's a heartbreaking reality at that. The Yorkshire Terrier Club of America is currently funding research into the genetic nature of the problem and investigating new paths in diagnosing and perhaps someday solving the problem.

In simple terms, the shunt is the means by which the fetus receives blood, food and oxygen from the mother. Normally, when the dog begins breathing on its own, the shunt disappears and the liver takes over. In other cases, this doesn't happen—for reasons yet unknown—and the liver does not develop normally, thereby leaving the dog in a situation that will eventually become life-threatening.

"In animals with portosystemic shunts, the blood bypasses the liver and is diverted to another blood vessel, allowing toxins to circulate through the body," says Dr. Jennifer Brinson, a veterinarian who specializes in internal medicine at the University of Illinois College of Veterinary Medicine Teaching Hospital in Urbana. The bypass of this blood flow creates a large amount of ammonia in the bloodstream.

Although most leading canine experts agree that shunts are genetic, there is also the possibility that they can develop later in life. Genetic shunts are generally diagnosed in dogs less than one year old. Acquired shunts can occur at any age and are often caused by liver disease. Shunts are also categorized as intra-hepatic (within the liver) or extrahepatic (outside the liver). According to Dr. Brinson, Yorkies have the tendency to have extrahepatic shunts in most cases.

Signs

Some signs of liver shunt may include listlessness, walking or running in circles, pressing the head down on surfaces, excessive drinking, frequent urination, lack of muscular coordination, coma, seizures, poor weight gain, sensitivity to sedatives (especially diaz-epam), depression, weakness, drooling, vomiting, poor appetite, and frequent urinary tract disease or early onset of bladder stones. If the signs of problems increase dramatically after eating, this is a strong indication of a liver shunt.

Diagnosis

Diagnosis of a suspected liver shunt is most often done in three stages. First the vet will check a blood and urine sample. If these samples suggest a shunt, second stage tests, consisting of a pre- and post-bile acid test and an ammonia challenge test, are performed. These two tests help determine the functional capacity of the liver. Recently the bile test has been questioned for Yorkshire Terriers since their normal bile levels tend to vary so much.

Finally, an ultrasound or nuclear scan may be used to try to locate and determine the extent of the shunt. Recent developments in the veterinary world have found that with the advent of Color Flow Ultrasound, a diagnosis can be made on non-anesthetized animals. Now this technology seems to be the diagnostic procedure of choice. If current research confirms its value, Color Doppler Ultrasound will soon be the preferred screening and diagnostic tool.

The Solution

The medical treatment for portosystemic shunts is aimed at reducing the amount of ammonia circulating in the body and decreasing the symptoms. A low-protein diet and lactulose to reduce absorption of ammonia are prescribed. In emergency cases, enemas with water or lactulose are used to reduce ammonia absorption immediately. If portosystemic shunts go untreated, the symptoms will get progressively worse and eventually the dog may die.

Treatment and prognosis of shunts depend on their location and severity. "A congenital, single, extrahepatic shunt that is caught early is a good candidate for surgery," says Dr. Brinson. Of course, some cases are not treatable and the dog must be euthanized to avoid unnecessary pain and suffering. Your vet can advise you of the options.

L'egg Perthes

Also called L'egg-Calve-Perthes (LCP), this is a disease of the hip joints typical to toy breeds. The head of the femur (the ball part of the ball and socket) starts to disintegrate, causing pain, limping, and, over time, arthritis. If your Yorkie has it, you will usually see it appear between 6-12 months. You can confirm the condition with x-rays. It usually occurs in one side only (as opposed to hip dysplasia which is generally bi-lateral).

Hip dysplasia is the deterioration and degeneration of the socket itself whereas L'egg Perthes is the degeneration of the ball. A fall or blow to the hip can cause swelling and cut off the flow of blood to the femoral head, triggering degeneration.

It is difficult, if not impossible, to know if L'egg Perthes is caused by trauma or genetic makeup, although both are possible. I don't allow puppies up on furniture until there are agile and big enough to get up on their own. Preventing jumps and falls during the first year is a good idea to avoid the trauma of L'egg Perthes later.

The Solution

Generally, L'egg Perthes is treated surgically by removing the head of the femur and letting the muscles form a "false joint." This acts to diminish the contact between bones at the hip joint. Fortunately, this surgery has excellent results although the recovery time can vary from dog to dog.

Mild cases may not require medical care. Just supervising the activity and forcing your Yorkie to rest may be enough to promote healing of the damaged areas, particularly if the cause is trauma and swelling in the socket.

Unfortunately, many dogs have advanced cases of L'egg Perthes by the time a veterinarian confirms the condition with x-rays and surgery is the only option. Recovery from this surgery can be slow with recovery periods of up to one year sometimes occurring before good use of the affected leg returns. If muscle atrophy is not present at the time of surgery, the recovery time is usually much less. Pain relief and anti-inflammatory medications may be beneficial.

However, it is not uncommon to see the muscles of the affected leg atrophy from disuse; the dog will naturally have had the tendency to keep weight off a leg that is hurting her. This can slow the recovery period considerably. Crazy as it sounds, water therapy, where the dog is actually swimming in a small pool or even a tub as part of the therapy, can work miracles. The benefit of using water to recover from this type of surgery is that the pressure that would normally be on the leg from walking is not there in the water.

Swimming forces the dog to use both rear legs rather than allowing the strong leg to dominate the physical activity. Dogs tend to learn quickly to walk on three legs and even when the problem is solved, the habits may remain.

Luxating Patellas

Translate "luxating" as "dislocating." The patella is your dog's "kneecap," the joint on the front of her hind leg. So a luxating patella is a dislocating, or trick kneecap, that keeps slipping out of its socket. I have seen this happen in Yorkies with weak ligaments, tendons, and/or muscles. It can also happen in Yorkies whose kneecap groove is too narrow or shallow. The dog's knee will usually slip inward, toward her body, and lock so that she can't bend her leg.

Occasionally this is caused by an injury, but overwhelming evidence shows that it is a genetic problem. You unfortunately have many breeders out there that breed only for money, not for the good of the breed. They don't care whether the dog has problems with its legs in the future; all they care about is their money. I know this because things like luxating patella and other genetic problems continue to be passed along through the Yorkie breed. There's only one way to stop it and that is not continuing to breed a dog with it in their line.

Another cause—the most common, in my opinion—is the skeletal structure of the rear "assembly" being cow-hocked. This can be caused by bowed leg bones (an 'S' curve) that do not correctly line up at the knee. The muscles and ligaments are not in a straight line from the crooked bones (femur and lower leg bone) above and below the knee. Therefore, the kneecap is pulled out of the groove it is supposed to glide in. Eventually the groove is worn smooth by the continual bad alignment.

Signs of luxating patella are if your Yorkie sometimes lifts one hind leg while she is running, or if she often moves both rear legs at the same time, like a hopping bunny.

Sometimes her knee slips only for a few moments, then slides back into place. The knee can also slip and stay out, and you will see a limping Yorkie that will hold her leg off the ground, perhaps tucking her thigh into her body and slipping to the outside or inside of the leg. You may have luxating patellas in one knee or in both. It is seen in both males and females, though it seems to be more common in females.

Types of Luxation
There are four basic degrees of luxating patellas:

1. The knee only slips out when the vet manipulates it. Don't let anyone force it out!

2. The knee luxates at times when your Yorkie is walking or running. She may not be that affected by it or she may cry, but it usually slides back by itself as she continues moving. You can also slip it back manually. Place your Yorkie on a level surface. Lace

both your hands over her stomach and gently slide your thumbs toward the dog's back legs, lifting her rear slightly into the air. As you are doing this, very gently slide your thumbs on to the dog's legs and straighten the legs out. You may hear a clicking noise as you do this, but don't be alarmed by it; that is the sound of the kneecap sliding back into place. This is the same process you use to evaluate if a dog is cow-hocked, If the leg bones don't line up straight, this could pre-dispose a puppy to luxating patella.

3. The knee slips out frequently, to the point of causing chronic lameness. Even when you put it back manually, it doesn't seem to last long. Your Yorkie may limp around on three legs for as little as a day or two or as much as a week, and is usually uncomfortable enough to be pretty inactive during that time.

4. The knee slips out of the socket and you cannot put it back in. This variety is pretty uncommon.

Traditional Solutions

Probably the best solution, at least initially—because luxating patella is so often a "wait and see" situation— is to limit activity. No jumping! However, there are traditional, veterinary solutions that you should at least be aware of:

- **Non-steroidal anti-inflammatory drugs**. This is the type of solution we would use for arthritis on ourselves. An example of a dog drug is Rimadyl. The trouble with these types of drugs is that they mask the symptoms, but don't actually strengthen or correct the knee in any way.

- **Steroidal anti-inflammatory drugs**. These can be damaging to the immune system, as well as procuring terrible side effects (in both the short and long term). They can also retard healing which you don't want if the problem is injury related. I don't recommend their use.

- **Surgery**. Surgery would be my absolute *last* resort and my least-given recommendation. The most typical surgery, and the one that has been the operation of choice for many years, is to go in and remove the cartilage from the joint. Then the vet literally deepens the groove that the knee bone goes into, replaces the cartilage and closes it up. I am against this method because it is invasive, painful and requires a lengthy recovery.

  The first two varieties of luxating patella don't even warrant surgery. You might elect to have the surgery performed for the fourth kind of luxation, or on the third type if it did not respond naturally. The costs for this surgery run about $500 per leg, it is tortuous for your Yorkie, and the failure rate is about 50 percent.

  Now there is a new surgery that is gentle and not very invasive where they run a long stitch around from the back of the knee around the kneecap and back to the rear again. They use a ligament material and this procedure provides a faster recovery. It does not invade any bones, is quick to do, and the recovery is much less painful than any of the previous types of surgeries.

  The strongest argument for this newer surgery is that if a dog continues to favor one leg and begins to use it exclusively, the added strain on the good leg—that is doing the work of two at this point—can injure the cruciate ligament on the good leg. Don't let one bad leg lead to injury of the good leg. Have the surgery to stabilize the patella and keep the dog using all four legs.

  Generally, I suggest that you look at the dog's activity to decide whether surgery is a good idea for you dog. If they are more sedentary you may not need to do any surgery at all. But if your little tiger is running, jumping, tearing around, you may want to talk to your veterinarian about this newer surgery. Other things to think about with your dog are heart conditions, liver and kidney function, breeding plans, age and so forth.

Natural Solutions

These options can not only be preventive, but also give some relief to a pre-existing case of luxating patella.

- The leaner your Yorkie is, the better, not only for overall health, but also because it puts less strain on the joints of a dog with luxating patellas.

- Even moderate exercise, for instance, walking up gentle slopes, can strengthen the muscle groups surrounding the patella.

- Feed fresh foods. Muscle, tissue and ligaments thrive on Vitamin C. The rice/chicken diet (see chapter 6) can work very well to supply your Yorkie with this and other necessary nutrients.

- There are products like Glyco-flex and Glucosamine that are packed with minerals, amino acids, enzymes, and lubricating agents. They claim to build cartilage and cushioning fluid in injured joints, and to be beneficial in healing damaged connective tissue. Generally I don't advocate this type of remedy, but if you are at your wit's end, I would suggest this over surgery any day. Check with your vet before beginning this type of treatment for dosage appropriate to your Yorkie's size.

HEART PROBLEMS

As with toy poodles, one of the major complications from reduction of size in Yorkies is the heart. If the internal support organs like the heart are reduced faster than the actual size of the outer structure like bones and overall size, the result can be a heart that cannot keep up with the body.

As the puppy grows, it is increasingly difficult for the smaller heart to function well enough to supply enough blood to the body and brain so it begins to enlarge to try to pump faster and move more blood. As the heart grows bigger and bigger to keep up with the growing puppy, it begins to put pressure on the lungs. Soon fluid from the heart starts seeping into the lungs, as the heart is not able to pump efficiently enough to move all the blood out into the bloodstream.

The symptoms are fluid on the lungs which diminishes the amount of oxygen that can be absorbed from the lungs. That makes the heart pump faster because it is not getting enough oxygen. It becomes a vicious circle that cannot be reversed. This puppy will ultimately collapse and have to be put down as with the hydrocephalic puppy (below).

These problems might not show up until these tinies are three to five months old. That is when they seem to go through their second growing spell. This is where the heart falls behind if it is going to. Some tiny Yorkies stay small enough that they don't fall into this situation. But when you buy a small or tiny Yorkie under five months old, you will not be able to tell if this puppy will stay small or literally outgrow their body organs.

HERNIAS

A hernia is a weakening or separation in the abdominal wall where internal tissue is able to protrude through the wall and form a bulge. There are two common areas where a hernia will occur: the groin (inguinal) and the navel (umbilical).

Umbilical or Navel Hernias

This type of hernia is most likely caused by pulling on the umbilical cord at the time of birth. You will see this in the "belly button" area. Usually small, these can be pushed in and then pop back out when the pressure subsides. Even though these are small and do not appear to be a problem, I advise that they be surgically repaired as soon as possible. When the puppy goes under anesthesia for removal of retained puppy teeth or for spaying or neutering, that is an opportune time to have this repaired. It only takes a few stitches to repair what is essentially a "hole" in the abdominal wall.

Inguinal or Groin Hernias

Seen in the groin area, these are holes in the abdominal wall that all puppies are born with to some extent. In some cases, the holes are too large or do not close normally. When the puppy is in a standing position, fatty tissue can slip through the hole and protrude from the abdominal wall.

This type of hernia can also be repaired and I recommend it, especially since they tend to get worse with age. Yorkies gain weight, putting more strain on the weakened tissue, and aggravating the situation. It is much less risky to alleviate this early when the dog is young and healthy.

Overall, for both types of hernias, if the hernia becomes "strangulated," a hard swelling that is painful to the dog will occur. This can be an emergency situation; consult your vet immediately.

HYDROCEPHALUS

If the brain continues to grow faster than the plates can spread and grow, pressure builds up from the fluid that flows into and out of the skull to nourish the brain tissue. As the expanding brain squeezes the vessels shut, fluid becomes trapped in the skull and cannot get out. The resulting pressure causes malfunction of the brain and you might see seizures, and/or hydrocephalus (water on the brain).

Symptoms include a glazed eye look, acting drunk, wobbly walking, etc. Because of the immediate and potential long-term damage to the puppy, I recommend putting the dog down. Refer to my section on open fontanels in this chapter for more information on how this starts.

OPEN FONTANELS

Open fontanels tend to occur most frequently in tiny Yorkies. I have seen it happen genetically in standard sized dogs as well. It also might happen when a breeder is breeding for a small muzzle, large eyes and a so-called baby doll face. If the skeletal structure is reduced faster than the brain, you have a skull that is too small for the brain.

Most puppies are born with a hairline separation at the center of their skull. In the case of open fontanels, the skull is in separate plates at birth that are not connected except by fibrous tissue like cartilage which must allow for the four plates to move and accommodate the brain as it grows. If the brain is too large for the skull, the plates will not join. There might be a small hole in the middle of the skull half way between the eyes and the ears that might never close up or calcify (become hard). This is similar to the soft spot on a newborn human baby.

A Yorkie with an open fontanel must be treated carefully, as she is particularly susceptible to head injuries that could be fatal. Refer to my section on Hydrocephalus in this chapter.

PARASITES

Internal

The biggest concerns in the area of internal parasites are tapeworms, roundworms, hookworms and coccidiosis.

Coccidiosis

This is an insidious infectious disease caused by coccidia—protozoan parasites that attack parts of the small intestines causing a bloody, mucus-filled diarrhea. Some fallacies about this problem are that it is caused by unclean conditions. This is wrong. Coccidiosis can be carried from yard to yard by infected birds, their droppings, feathers, and flies. People can track it in on their shoes from walking in areas where it is present. Chicken yards and farm animal yards might have it as well. Don't let the misunderstandings about this problem keep you from taking prompt action. Coccidiosis kills, but is treatable if detected in time.

Diagnosis is achieved by taking a small stool sample to your veterinarian and in a few minutes he can determine if coccidiosis is present.

There is no "cure" for coccidiosis, (not even bleach will kill it), but rather puppies must develop a resistance to it. Coccidiosis is an opportunist; the puppy might handle it for a while, but when stress from shots, weaning, traveling, change of food or water, teething, etc. weaken the pup's resistance, then the coccidiosis takes over and can kill quickly. Adults may carry it and never exhibit any symptoms because they have immunity to this infectious problem, although it is not impossible for an adult to show symptoms.

The Solution

The product that has worked the most effectively for me is Nitrofurazone powder (4.1%); double strength needs to be diluted twice as much. You can find this at feed stores and drugstores that carry animal supplies; expect to pay about $8.00 per one pound bag of powder. Give 1/8 teaspoon per 5 pounds twice each day for three weeks. This dose must be cut down respectively for puppies and smaller dogs. This is a fairly safe product and has been used safely on young pups.

Nitrofurazone is easily administered in lean, raw hamburger meat, rolled in a tiny ball and the powder hidden the middle. In cases where the pup has such severe diarrhea that the medication goes through them so quickly and it doesn't have time to work, I mix it in a raw egg yolk and water mixture (one teaspoon of water per egg yolk). This allows the medication to stick to the insides better and gives quicker results. Then give 1/8 teaspoon Nitrofurazone powder (again in the per 5 pound measurement) plus one egg yolk plus one teaspoon of water for a mixture that is simple to administer.

In small puppies or young Yorkies, Albon (Sulfadimethoxine oral suspension 5%—also available in tablet form) may also be used with success. I start with two doses the first two days (1/4 cc per pound per dose) and then drop to one dose per day for the remainder of the three-week period. In some dogs, sensitivity to sulfa drugs may make this medication unacceptable.

PARASITES

Hookworms

These are less common than tapeworms and round-worms in the US, but they still are important to be aware of. You'll see them in the southern parts of the US in particular or in crowded areas where conditions are unsanitary.

A sure sign of hookworm is a black, tarry-looking stool and pale gums. Your vet can advise you on a diagnosis and solution.

Roundworms

Passed by the mother at birth, these worms resemble long strands of spaghetti and may wiggle when they are voided in feces. If the case is serious, you can see outer signs like an enlarged stomach, poor weight gain and diarrhea or vomiting. These parasites strike pup-pies between a few weeks old and a few months. Your veterinarian can diagnose them with an examination of the stools and can advise you on a treatment.

Tapeworms

This parasite lives and grows in the small intestine. Usually acquired by the dog eating fleas, you will see very obvious outward signs of them. Look around the anus or in the stool and you will see things that look like either maggots or pieces of white rice.

This is not a life-threatening problem, but over time

it can wear the dog out because the worms are essentially "stealing" nutrients from the dog. One dog eating the stools of the infested dog cannot transfer the worms from dog to dog either.

Chemical treatment is the most common solution to this and takes care of the problem in most cases. Your vet can provide you with the necessary medication. I have also seen cases where giving the dog chopped garlic for a few days drives the worms out of the intestine.

SEIZURES

Seizures are a lapse of consciousness in the normal sense. The episodes can vary from staring absently with a fixed gaze to collapsing with body tremors. Usually the Yorkie knows that it is about to happen and will come to your side and want to be very close to you. After the seizure, which can last either a few minutes or as long as an hour, your Yorkie may be very weak and listless. Her limbs may not seem to work properly and she may have to be helped from place to place.

Seizures can be triggered by many different things: injuries to head, reduced size of head, stress—according to what vets have told me, dogs can have the tendency for seizures under extreme pain, stress or emotional upheaval. There can also be physical reasons for seizures, such as genetics, metabolic imbalance, disorders like liver shunt, structural conditions like open fontanels or head injuries.

The Solution

Typically, seizures are treated with a drug called

Phenobarbitol, but I would not advise treating a dog with this drug unless the seizures became so frequent and so severe as to interfere with the dog's quality of life.

During the actual seizure, you can do several things. First and foremost, get your Yorkie out of harm's way. She will not be able to control herself, so pick her up and hold her if that is what it takes to keep her safe. Next, think about whether anything triggered this seizure. Was there an unusual stress? Did you or the vet just administer medication or did the dog fall or jump and hit her head?

Your next action is to have the vet examine her, especially if this is the first seizure she has had. That way, he can rule out anything that obviously was the cause.

If there is nothing external that caused the seizure, I advise that you keep track of how often your Yorkie has seizures and how long they last.

Above all, this can be harder on us emotionally as humans than it actually is on the dog. We find it difficult to have to stand by helplessly and be unable to help our little friend. The best thing you can do is to hold her and speak soothingly to her. Just try to keep her as comfortable as possible until she gets through it.

I always consider the dog's quality of life the primary priority, so as long as your Yorkie has a happy, pain-free existence on a daily basis, then you probably don't need drugs to control the seizures. If the seizures become a daily or even weekly event, you need to take that into consideration.

SPAY/NEUTER

I believe wholeheartedly that if you get a Yorkie for companion purposes, you will be much happier with this pet if it is spayed or neutered. Spaying is the term for removing the uterus of females and neutering is the  removal of male testicles (and sometimes the cutting of the cords to the testicles rather than removal) for the purpose of eliminating the possibility of either re-producing. Some people have reservations and are worried about changing the dog's temperament or taking some of the sparkle out of their step.

Spaying Your Female

One of the reasons I recommend the spaying of fe-males is that if they are not spayed and continue to come into heat every six months for years on end, there is an increasing risk that they will develop a pyometra. This is an infection that occurs in dogs where a hor-monal imbalance happens at the same time as an e-coli bacterial infection. This uterine infection is very diffi-cult to detect and diagnose until sometimes it is too late. It is life-threatening and in most cases can only be treated by immediate emergency spaying. This sur-gery is much more dangerous with the infection in progress (instead of spaying while they are not having any problems) as they can go into shock during the surgery itself. Great care must be taken to treat with aggressive antibiotic therapy, and prepare against shock. The nature of the infection itself lends itself to shock if the blood supply is touched by the infection during surgery.

As I've stated, in my opinion, the e-coli infection occurs first and then brings on the hormonal imbalance as a result of the infection, causing a pyometra as a side effect. This situation can never happen if the female is spayed. It is better to do this while the bitch is young enough to have surgery rather than waiting until she is past her prime and might have other health issues that would make surgery too risky.

If you spay after your female has begun going into heat, try to time the spay between heat cycles so that the female organs are at their smallest size. Otherwise there is extra swelling and heavy blood flow that is common during heat cycles. She will have a faster recovery with less chance of danger and complications as well.

Neutering Your Male

There are many different opinions about neutering your male dog, regardless of the breed. Yorkies are particularly territorial since they have a terrier nature to begin with. Add male hormones to the package and it gets more difficult to curb the male territorial dominance that shies people away from male puppies.

I would generally say that if the male dog is the only dog your house and he will not be exposed to other animals—not even ones that visit—or if you never plan to get another dog, then you don't have to neuter him. Not having any of the above factors pretty much rules out the reasons that male dogs have gotten such a bad reputation for marking and those are competition and territoriality.

Some male Yorkies can be trained to a point, but why go through all of that? Neutering your male will make it easier for you to house train him, it will curb his tendency to run away, and he will be less likely to chase or search for females. If he is not being used for breeding, you will have a better pet overall if you neuter him.

I recommend that the neutering take place before or around six months of age, before the aggressive/dominant behaviors have the opportunity to set in. Some male puppies start to lift their rear leg to urinate by three or four months. To take an adult male and neuter him will not change his behavior patterns.

Non-Invasive Spay/Neuter

In years past I always recommended that people wait until at least six months on males and eight months on females (depending on size) before doing surgeries. This was to reduce the chance of complications (mostly from the anesthesia). I usually advised that when you have puppy teeth removed, it was a good time to spay or neuter so that the dog only went under anesthesia once instead of twice. This tooth removal is usually done around eight or nine months as most of the puppy teeth have been replaced by permanent teeth by then.

Now there is a new approach. This is exciting because it is "non-invasive," meaning there is no surgery required. An injection is made either into the testicles or the uterus, simply retarding the development of the reproductive organs. What is wonderful about this new procedure is that no anesthesia is required, it appears to render them permanently sterile, and can be done on young puppies as early as three months old. In addition, it is less expensive and requires relatively no recovery time. This is a great breakthrough for people with a limited income, for small dogs/puppies that would be a surgical risk, for puppies that the breeder wants to be absolutely sure will never be bred even by mistake, and for people that are generally squeamish about surgeries.

The veterinary world has embraced this new procedure as a possible solution to the overpopulation of the canine species. This new way of eliminating the breeding capability can be especially helpful for people who adopt animals from shelters. By giving the dog the injection before releasing them, the shelters are assured that it gets done before they leave for their new home.

This injection procedure is especially valuable to toy breeds like Yorkies which have so many pitfalls with surgeries and anesthesia.

VACCINATIONS

You do have the choice of giving vaccinations yourself or allowing the vet to give them. No matter who gives the shots, make sure an adequate amount of time is allowed between each shot to give the immune system time to recover. Never give any vaccination if a puppy or an adult is under the weather in any way. That means worms, diarrhea, vomiting, not eating, injury, coughing, etc. Keep this in mind: you are introducing a disease—whether it be a virus, bacteria or whatever—for the purpose of fighting it, so let's take *one stress at a time.*

Make sure your puppy has eaten before shots or at least make sure they eat right afterwards to avoid hypoglycemia brought on by stress.

Reactions

Watch for reactions to the shot for at least two to three hours afterward, whether they are given by you or by the vet. If you see any signs of pale or grey gums, weakness, trembling, hives, red splotches, excessive itching, swollen eyelids, coughing, vomiting, diarrhea, or collapse, take immediate action. I keep epinephrine in the refrigerator with syringes ready to use. I also keep Benadryl liquid and tablets, as well as dexamethasone (the anti-shock drug) in both injectible and tablet form.

To judge whether to use a pill or a needle, use the oral treatment for less severe reactions and the needle for more severe ones. The sooner the reaction occurs, the more impact it may have and the more severe it can become. Get on the phone to the vet as soon as you see the first signs of trouble; you are only the nurse—they are the doctors!

If You Give Your Own Shots

One trick is to give puppies and adults one-fourth of a baby aspirin about one half hour before combination shots. I try to be sure they have eaten prior to shots, too. For those of you who give your own shots, my vet taught me that they are much less painful if given in the rib area behind the shoulder blades. If you give them at the back of the neck or in front of the shoulder blades, there are glands there and the shot can be very painful.

I give the shots sub-cutaneous about one inch to the

right or left of the spine and behind the shoulders about one inch. They hardly ever have a painful reaction. If the dog seems to react strongly when the needle goes in, before the medication is even injected, chances are you have hit a nerve and its better to withdraw the needle and start over in another spot. I always clean the top of the vials with alcohol, but I make sure it is totally dry before I withdraw the shot.

Parvo

Parvo vaccinations are "immune suppressing" for 10 days after the shot. The next 10 days after that are needed for the dog to multiply its antibodies and build its immune system. Many years ago when I was learning things the hard way, my sister and I did the "every 10 days" shot routine and had four pups come down with parvo at 16 weeks because their immune systems were totally suppressed by shots that were given too frequently. They had no defense at all.

Therefore, I recommend that parvo shots be spaced out between three to four weeks apart. Also, I recommend that you do not give a shot before traveling or having an exposure as it will only make them more susceptible to coming down with an illness.

If the puppy is at high risk due to traveling or exposure it is better to give a *killed parvo vaccination* instead of *modified live parvo vaccine.* This is because the killed vaccine is *not immune suppressing* while the *modified live virus* is immune suppressing.

Rabies

When you give several vaccinations at a time, you divide the army of antibodies between the number of organisms that are given. To give a rabies vaccination at the age of 12 weeks means you are diverting a portion of the immune system from the killer (parvo, for instance) to a virus (rabies) that exposure to is very unlikely. You diminish the number of antibodies available to protect from a very common virus that is also a killer of puppies. Not good.

Another reason I would not give rabies at 12 weeks is that 12 weeks is the time when many if not most puppies are in the "window." This is the greatest risk time for pups as their mother's antibodies that they got at birth are almost gone (used up by the earlier "puppy shots," and the pups own immune system have not really had enough time to develop sufficiently to protect the puppy.

Only your vet should give the rabies vaccinations. It is a disease that humans can contract and therefore needs special handling.

I recommend the "sub-q" (sub-cutaneous, meaning under the skin) type of vaccination for rabies. The reason is that the IM (intra-muscular, meaning in the muscle) shot is too severe and traumatic for small dogs.

Chapter 11

The Culture Program

For those of you who are unfamiliar with the term "pathogenic," it is a term that is applied to bacteria that cause infection in the host. Bacteria are everywhere and most are harmless to their hosts. But sometimes when bacteria are subjected to an antibiotic, they can develop a resistance or tolerance for that antibiotic or others, particularly if the antibiotic is only used for three or four days and then discontinued.

The purpose of an antibiotic is not to "cure," in the traditional sense of the word. The purpose is to slow the infection down long enough for the host's—in this case, you or your Yorkie—immune system to take over. When the symptoms seem to be diminishing, there is the tendency to stop taking the medication, thinking "What a wonderful drug, the dog is better in three days!" Actually, as soon as the medication is withdrawn, the bacteria bounce back with renewed vigor and a resistance to that particular drug. In light of this new, stronger bacteria, a different medication must now be used to fight the bacteria because the first drug is no longer effective.

When this pattern is repeated a few times, a "super germ" is created that is now resistant to many of the common antibiotics and is capable of causing serious problems to the host. If it is causing symptoms, then it is called "pathogenic."

What to Do

When your Yorkie is sick and you cannot identify the illness, the first thing that must be done is to identify the bacteria. This is done by your vet taking a sample, or culture, of the bacteria (either vaginal on bitches or the prepuce on males, or any area that appears infected, such as eyes, ears or wounds) and sending it to a laboratory. Once the lab identifies it, they should run a sensitivity test. This means that about ten antibiotics are used to test the bacteria to determine if the bacteria continues to grow (Resistant) or is slowed down (Sensitive) by each antibiotic.

If ten antibiotics are tested and the bacteria is "sensitive" to four or five, then it might be non-pathogenic. If, on the other hand, the bacteria is "resistant" to seven or eight out of the ten tested, then this bacteria has a greater chance of being or becoming pathogenic. It is only considered "pathogenic" if the patient is exhibiting symptoms of a problem.

The reason all this is so important is that if you just take an antibiotic from your vet and give it to your Yorkie, it could mask the real symptoms of what is going on. Sometimes antibiotics are given to protect from complications such as pneumonia, when a stressed dog might be at risk; this is known as a prophylactic. In most cases, you can't just take an antibiotic and use it as a blanket, crossing your fingers that it will address whatever is wrong with your dog.

During antibiotic therapy, and for a week afterward, you should give fresh yogurt and acidophilus every day in the dog's diet. This, hopefully, will replace pathogenic bacteria with good bacteria like bacillus. If you eliminate all bacteria from the vaginal tract or other areas, you open the door for a yeast infection.

When the bacteria that is present during medication is eliminated, it opens the door for whatever opportunistic pathogenic bacteria (sometimes even worse than what you started with) to move into the system. It's kind of like "rental" property. Something will try to live there: good bacteria, pathogenic bacteria, or yeast. So provide a source of good bacteria if you must medicate.

I have studied extensively in the area of zoonotic diseases (passed from animal to human or vice versa) and bacterial infections. In doing so, I have found that our problem of fading puppy syndrome (weak puppies that eventually just "fade" health-wise and die) as well as infertility among bitches can be attributed to bacterial infections in most of the cases.

My Culture Program

If veterinarians would routinely run a culture first and then start the most likely antibiotic while waiting for the culture results, many dogs and puppies would be saved. So often the antibiotic will be given, you go home and start the dog on it, then end up coming back to the vet—that is, if the dog survives. Then you end up trying yet another antibiotic that is most likely chosen by chance rather than by virtue of a culture with sensitivities and resistances.

By the time a culture is taken, the wrong antibiotics might be in the system and alter the readings of the culture, obscuring or slowing the true results. You have to realize that in this day and age, the bacteria are becoming more and more resistant to the old standby antibiotics that medicine has gotten so comfortable with over the last 50 years. The administration of antibiotics has become a knee jerk response instead of a carefully reasoned, tested response to an illness.

How Does This Affect You?

Dogs are carriers of various microbes, both good and bad. The problem arises when humans become contagious to their dogs. In other words, you can give your Yorkie an infection and the dog may not be affected by it, but she will carry it to other humans or other pets who *will*. My solution to this is that if you are sick for any reason, isolate yourself from your Yorkie just as you would from a baby.

Maybe you have gotten a puppy from a breeder that had infection running through the whole litter. Your puppy could be seriously ill and just surviving by chance. She may have been on medication, but the breeder didn't tell you. This puppy is susceptible to other dogs and humans who are sick, and the puppy may need your help.

Those of you who want a tiny Yorkie need to know that, sometimes, tiny puppies are that size because they're sick. Fading puppies don't gain weight, are passive, sickly and stress-prone. The infection can be lying there in wait until a stress comes and then when the infection rears up, you have a dog in complete crisis, with an immune system unable to deal with the simplest things like teething, shots or travel.

Take the most obvious precautions. You can bring disease home to your dog; wash your hands if you have been near other dogs or just out in the world for a while. Wash your hands after you go to the bathroom. Think about where you are going to have your Yorkie groomed, if you do.

If someone in the family is sick or visiting a sick person, don't let your Yorkies have direct contact with this person until he or she is well. For yourself, don't take your Yorkie to bed with you when you have strep throat.

Bacteria have a way of sharing information with each other and becoming "super germs." Bacteria can become drug-resistant and pathogenic just by associating with other bacteria. They evolve very quickly.

If you expose your Yorkie to illness or disease, be it animal or human, there can be a transference of resistances and pathogenicity that can develop into disease later on.

Chapter 12

Saying Goodbye

Thadius was an outrageously willful puppy we all called the Tazmanian Devil. He had dignity and self-awareness from day one when I brought him home under my shirt (after being born C-section at the vet). He never backed off to any dog and I was forced to put up a fence when he chased a German Shepherd half a block to the neighbors at the age of one.

It is hard to express how profoundly grateful a human can be to a little five-pound dog, but "Thadius" truly changed my life.

I bought his mother based on her pedigree, incredibly inbred on Champion Wildweir Fair N' Square, and drove through mountain blizzards to breed her to American/Canadian Champion Bluecreek Chili Pepper, a Champion Kajimanor Olde Spice son. I was just starting in Yorkshires and knew that this was an important breeding. I wanted to stay in the bloodline that I had researched to be the foundation stock behind every dog that I liked when I reviewed all the magazines.

In my first year of breeding, I had four litters, a total of six puppies born, and Thadius was the only puppy to live. My first home bred Yorkshire Terrier became my first homebred Champion and sire of twenty champions. His attitude, showmanship, charm, stamina, heart, loyalty and trust of his human family (including many people spanning the USA) are some of the wonderful traits that make him impossible to forget.

I must say to the world that his biggest win and my proudest moment was when he won the YTCA and YTCGNY Stud Dog Classes with his beloved Champion Lemire's Peeping Tom and Champion Lemire's Oh My Belinda Blue at the age of seven in New York.

I suppose some people can handle the loss of a pet with a certain ease. They keep an emotional barrier between themselves and the animals. I cannot do this. I can only keep a pet if I form a bond with him or her. There has the be that special chemistry—magic, really— between us.

My Thadius taught me so many things about dignity and self essence. He taught me that his rights were equal to mine in his eyes. He gave me total trust and never held back. He didn't question my control when it came to important things. We held a bond of love that was so strong, I can still feel it.

I had Thadius for a wonderful 15˙ years. In the last couple of months, he began to get weaker. I could tell he was exhausted because he didn't jump up to harass me when I came home, as was his habit. He would not spring to his feet when I entered the room; he would only open an eye to see if I was coming his way.

I always hoped that he would choose his own time and let go, maybe in the night during a dream. But after a few months of his downhill trend, I knew that he was hanging on just for me. He didn't want to let me down. He was my sentinel, my guardian, my soulmate. He wouldn't abandon his post and leave me alone, no matter how much pain he was in.

As he got worse and worse, he couldn't see me anymore, and when I called him, he couldn't walk the two feet into my arms. Seeing him confused, arthritic, uncoordinated and weak was more than I could bear for him.

I called my vet and arranged for him to come to the house on a certain day. I wanted time to say goodbye. I wanted Thadius to be bathed and have some quality time with me and with his family.

On the night before he was to go, I let him have all his favorite goodies, including doggie ice cream and his favorite cookie treats. I was fortunate that a dear friend was willing to come and hold Thadius in her arms since I couldn't do it. I know he understands that I couldn't; I needed to remember him alive. He gave me a last lick and we got some precious pictures together before I let him go.

You see, I had made Thadius a promise when he was

just a young pup that I would never let him suffer. I would not force him to continue on if life hurt him. He trusted me to keep my word even when it hurt me to let him go.

With Thadius I had the chance to talk to him about it and tell him what was going on. My sister told me to ask him if he was ready and that he would tell me with his look. She was right. I told him exactly what was going to happen and that all of us loved him. I asked him to let me know if it was okay or if he wasn't ready. He told me he was so tired and that if I could help him he was ready.

Sometimes we lose a pet by accident or at the vet's with no notice. That is very different and no less difficult. I know now that all my sweet Yorkies, including Thadius, who is back in charge of the pack just as he was here on earth, are playing and running.

I will forever feel grateful and amazed that I was privileged to breed and own this noble Yorkie who taught me so much about life and love.

Easing Your Pain

Obviously, losing your best friend is a loss just as losing a human friend is. There is no way you can replace your Yorkie just by getting another one. One way that you can ease the transition, however, is to get another Yorkie before the older one dies.

You can do this with an older dog or you can choose to have a pair of Yorkies from the beginning. I have seen it work very well for someone who has a Yorkie that is say, ten years old to bring in a puppy. I have also had people who have a two year old Yorkie bring in a puppy and that can work, too.

WHEN YOU'RE GONE

You should have a game plan about what you want to happen to your dogs if something happens to you. I advise that you put something in your will about this, especially who you want to oversee the distribution and care of your animals if you are not around to do so.

Dogs that I co-own with someone, I have already made out AKC transfer slips and signed them, to be filled out and sent in, in the event of my death. They are in my safe with my will.

You should have contracts and instructions complete if you have specific desires that you want followed. Copies of these should be on file with AKC, in your folder so that they will not hold up the transfer of dogs if you are gone.

Identify Your Yorkies

It is important that dogs be easily identifiable to other people if you are not around to tell them apart. Tattoos are great for this purpose. I recommend registering them with a tattoo registry to help protect from stealing and help them come back to you if lost.

There is a new type of identification by use of a microchip that is implanted under the skin that is becoming more common. I don't know how I feel about this method at this time, but you might want to research this method for your situation and its availability in your area. My understanding, however, is that shelters and humane societies look for microchips and will not euthanize a dog that has one implanted. Start with talking to your veterinarian and local dog clubs.

Letting Go With Love

There are times that it is kinder to have a dog euthanized in the event of your death for various reasons. If the dog's health or age would not allow for a comfortable transition to a new home, or if they are not housebroken (leading to potential abuse in a new home), you may decide this is best.

My deceased dogs are cremated and I will be, too. Then when I am gone, their ashes will be scattered in a special place with my own ashes.

TRUSTS AND WILLS

Your Yorkie needs to be taken care of if something happens to you just as you take care of her while you are alive. How can you make sure that your Yorkie is well taken care of if something—death, sickness, etc.—happens to you?

Your will needs to clearly delineate where you want your Yorkie to go in the case of your death. This means you are planning in advance, with the agreement of someone else, whether it is a friend or relative, for the care of your Yorkie. Name at least two people just in case.

Another thing to be sure of is that there is money allocated in your will for the care of your dog. This bypasses the whole idea of leaving money to your dog, which legally doesn't work. Instead, you can name the designated caretaker and delineate how the money is to be used.

You may also decide to establish a trust in your Yorkie's name. Of course, you still need to name a trustee to manage the care and expenditure of the money. You would deposit cash or cash equivalents in this trust.

Then by law, the person that you designate as your trustee must look after the dog.

Not all states allow pet trusts; check with your local government or an attorney to be sure. In addition, your trust is taxable. Keep those kinds of things in mind when deciding between a will and a trust.

Rainbow Bridge Return
by Joy LaCaille

The little dog arrived at the Rainbow Bridge, and a pack of dogs rushed up to greet him. He braced himself, expecting a fight, but this was the first pack that wagged their tails and kissed him instead of attacking him.

It was beautiful here, and everyone was nice to him. None of them had been born in a puppy mill, like he had, and used for dog-bait fighting and left to die in a shelter because he was a mix-breed battle-scarred cur and wasn't cute. They explained why they were waiting for their humans who loved them.

"What is love?" he asked, and God let him go back to earth and find out. Warm, and dark, he squeezed in with the others and waited for the day to be born. Scared, he held back as long as he could, but finally got dragged out, by his hind feet. Hands without fur held him gently and rubbed him dry and opened his mouth and guided him to a warm nipple with milk. He didn't get a good hold on it, because one of his big fat brothers pushed him aside. The human hand moved the other puppy to another nipple and held his body, so he could drink.

"Ahhh, that's better, " he thought, and drank until his jaws got tired and he curled up to sleep next to his warm hairy mother. "I remember this," he mused... "Too bad I'll have to grow up to be hit, left out in the cold and rain, and used for dog-bait fighting, and die as an unclaimed rescue dog. I remember what it's like, being a dog." he thought sadly.

That night, he crawled up to his mother and tried to nurse, but he kept getting pushed off to the side. When they were full, the big brothers and sisters got their bottoms cleaned and he finally latched on to a nipple, but the human hands weren't there to hold him up, and there wasn't any milk in any of the nipples, anyway. He was weak and so tiny. It was even hard to stay upright, and he fell over on his back and couldn't right himself.

So he began to cry, and suddenly the human hands were there, holding him up and putting a rubber thing in his mouth. It didn't taste or feel like mother, but it was warm and made the ache in his tummy go away.

He was having trouble breathing, as his lungs weren't fully developed, because he had waited too long to join the others in the womb, as he took one last romp at the Rainbow Bridge. He could feel the heartbeat of the human, who had laid him on her chest and covered him with a soft cloth, keeping him warm, and soothing his bony body with gentle circling touches.

He kept thinking of his new friends who had been so nice to him at the bridge and asked God if he could go back. God said, "Yes, but not just yet. You wanted to experience Love."

So for several hours (seemed like days but it was dark and he couldn't tell what time it was), the human supplemented his feeding and let him experience the warmth of his mother's body and tongue, and the pile of warm soft littermates. He got weaker, and the human held him more often, leaving the littermates to sleep in a pile while he got caressed, kissed, and got to listen to the heartbeat which was strong and loving.

Finally God came back and asked, "are you ready to come back to the Rainbow Bridge?"

"Yes, he responded," with a little sorrow, because the human didn't want to let him go, and was crying. He pushed the air out of his lungs and floated back to the Rainbow Bridge and looked back at the human, who was still crying and holding the limp body that he had borrowed for his trip.

"Thank you, God," he said. "Love is beautiful, and I will wait near the Bridge and let the human know, when she arrives, that I loved her, too."

Appendix 1

Poisonous Plants
Dog Drug List

POISONOUS PLANTS

The following is a list of plants that
can be poisonous to your Yorkie.

Aloe Vera
Fox Glove
Amarylis
Fruit and Nut Trees
Asparagus Fern
Geranium
Autumn Crocus
Golden Chain
Avocado
Hibiscus
Azalea
Holly
Begonia, Sand
Holly Berry
Bird of Paradise
Horsechestnut
Black Nightshade Berry
Hyacinth
Butterfly Weed
Hydrangea Blossom
Calla Lily
Iris
Catamonkin Orange Tree
Jack-in-the-Pulpit
Carnation
Jequirity Bean
Castor Bean
Jerusalem Cherry
Christmas Cherry
Jimson Weed
Cyclamen
Juniper
Daffodil
Larkspur
Daisy
Laurel

Daphne
Lily-of-the-Valley
Dead Nightshade
Mistletoe
Devil's Ivy
Morning Glory
Dieffenbachia
Needlepoint Ivy
Dumb Cane
Nightshade
Easter Lily
Oleander
English Holly/
Oxaias
English Ivy
Philodendron
Elderberry
Podocarpus
Elephant Ears
Poinsettia
Eucalyptus
Poison Ivy
Eyebane
Poison Sumac
Firecracker
Potato Plant
Pothos
Tomato Leaves
Pyrocantha
Tulips-Dermatitis
Rhododendron
Vegetables
Rhubarb
Violet Seeds
Schefflera
Wild Carrots

Skunk Cabbage
Wild Cucumber
Snow-on-the-Mountain
Wild Parsnip
Spathe Flower
Wild Peas
String of Pearls
Yew Tree
Tobacco
Here are some effects of poisoning by certain plants, taken from *277 Secrets Your Dog Wants You To Know* by Paulette Cooper and Paul Noble.

ALOE VERA: diarrhea, change of urine color to red

AMARYLLIS: vomiting

ASPARAGUS FERN: might cause allergic dermatitis

AUTUMN CROCUS: the leaves cause vomiting and nervous stimulation

AVOCADO: vomiting, diarrhea, and possible death

AZALEA: depression of the central nervous system and cardiovascular collapse

BIRD OF PARADISE: gastrointestinal disorders, vertigo

CYCLAMEN: vomiting, gastrointestinal problems, death

DAFFODIL: convulsions, vomiting, arrhythmia

DIEFFENBACHIA PLANTS: the various dieffenbacha plants can cause oral irritation, leading to suffocation

DUMB CANE: see "Dieffenbachia Plants"

EASTER LILY: kidney failure

FRUIT AND NUT TREES: like apple, peach, almond, cherry, apricot, which have stems and leaves with traces of cyanide

HIBISCUS: gastrointestinal reactions

HOLLY: vomiting, diarrhea, and central nervous system depression

HYDRANGEA: similar to fruit trees

LILY OF THE VALLEY: cardiac failure

MISTLETOE: cardiac problems

NIGHTSHADE: solanine in plant causes salivation, anorexia, gastrointestinal disturbance, depression

PHILODENDRON: calcium oxalate crystals lead to

oral and gastrointestinal
irritation
POINSETTIA: irritating to
mouth, stomach, and
possibly the heart
RHUBARB: leaves can kill
dogs
SCHEFFLERA: see "Philo-
dendron"
TOBACCO: leaves and
stems contain solanine,
same as "Nightshade"
VEGETABLES: such as
eggplant, mushrooms,
toadstools, and potatoes,
may cause vomiting and
diarrhea

 The ASPCA has an ex-
panded list of poisonous
plants on their website,
www.caninetimes.com.

A VERY BRIEF OVERVIEW OF ANIMAL DRUGS

ANESTHETICS
Anesthetics act to knock the dog unconscious, as for surgical or dental procedures.

SEDATIVES
Sedatives do what they sound like: sedate. In a way it is a form of unconsciousness but the brain patterns are not as deep as with an anesthetic.

PAIN KILLERS
Pain killers mean that the dog is awake but feeling little or no pain.

EXAMPLE: Torbugesic is a pain killer and cough suppressant considered standard practice in the last 10 to 15 years. Used frequently for dental procedures as a pre-anesthetic both to calm the animal and to reduce the pain experienced after the procedure, especially in the case of tooth extractions. Called a pre-anesthetic "cocktail" since its effect is to block different avenues in the brain. Beneficial in terms of cutting down the amount of anesthetic necessary during the procedure. It comes in a tablet and injection form. The tablet is considered less certain in terms of control and most vets seem to prefer the injection. They can tell when it gets to the peak blood level and therefore when it becomes most effective, as well as being able to control how much goes into the dog.

TRANQUILIZERS
Tranquilizers have a calming effect; this is emotional not physical.

EXAMPLE: Acepromazine is one of the most commonly used tranquilizers in veterinary medicine. It causes tranquilization and also has an anti-emetic effect. This makes it especially useful for treating car sickness, since that is often a combination of fear and motion sickness in dogs.

The recommended dosage for acepromazine is 0.25mg to 1mg per pound of body weight. In most cases it is not necessary to use the higher dosages unless you are trying to control fear based aggression. Acepromazine is considered to be very safe. The average toxic dose is significantly higher than the recommended dosage (at least 20 times the dose).

Despite this, acepromazine does have some significant effects that must be considered. It can cause hypotension (lowering of blood pressure). In addition, acepromazine seems to make it easier for dogs with seizure disorders to have a seizure.

Acepromazine doesn't have any pain-killing effects. **[Encyclopedia of Canine Veterinary Medical Information]**

Appendix 2

Breeder Contract

Purchase Agreement
(see notes at bottom)

The following agreement is between _____, hereafter referred to as "Breeder" and _____, hereafter referred to as "Purchaser."

In consideration of a purchase price of _____dollars ($), the breeder transfers in fee simple rights, privileges and responsibilities associated with the ownership of the (Male/Female) puppy of the Yorkshire Terrier breed as specified in the following, to purchaser as of the date specified below. Purchaser has the right to return the puppy to Breeder during the first 5 business days from the date of signature of this agreement for a refund in the amount of the purchase price, for any congenital or chronic medical condition certified by a licensed veterinarian and by breeder's veterinarian.

Breeder will remain as Co-Owner on this puppy until such time as it is spayed/neutered by a licensed veterinarian. Upon presentation by the purchaser of a Certificate of Spay/Neuter for this dog to the Breeder (or possible first hand examination of puppy/dog), Breeder will have her name removed as Co-Owner for this dog with no further cost or payment.

This Puppy is sold under limited registration as defined by The American Kennel Club. This is identical to Full Registration with the exception of litter registration privileges. No litters produced by the breeding of this dog will be accepted by the American Kennel Club for registration. Accordingly, any breeding of this puppy/dog will result in an unregisterable litter and will be deemed a serious violation of this contract and dealt with as outlined below.

Further, Purchaser agrees that should breeding occur with this puppy/dog, whether incidental or deliberate, ownership of this puppy/dog will revert to Breeder and Purchaser will return the puppy/dog to Breeder. Puppy/dog will be returned to Breeder the fastest way possible that will not endanger the life, welfare or well-being of the puppy/dog. All expenses incurred for the return of the puppy/dog as well as any expense that may be incurred by

Breeder for medical treatment or maintenance will be the responsibility of Purchaser.

Should Purchaser decide to relinquish ownership of this puppy/dog at any time during its life for any reason other than those directed by law, Purchaser agrees to return puppy/dog to Breeder as fast as possible by safest means possible that will not endanger the life, welfare or well-being of puppy/dog. All costs incurred for the return of the puppy/dog as well as any expense resulting from medical treatment and/or training, reconditioning or socialization will be the responsibility of Purchaser. This puppy/dog may not be sold, placed or in any means ownership relinquished to another party unless agreed upon by Breeder and expressed in writing by Breeder to Purchaser. If at any time Purchaser is unable or unwilling to provide for this puppy/dog it must be returned to Breeder under the terms specified above.

Should Purchaser or any household member be charged with animal cruelty/abuse or any act that is contrary to humane and responsible treatment of animals, this puppy's ownership will revert to Breeder. The same applies should any member of the house (renters included) be found to engage in breeding companion animals for profit or as any form of commerce/brokering or other third party sales arrangements.

Purchaser is responsible for:

a) keeping this puppy/dog up to date on all immunizations
b) annual check up by a licensed veterinarian,
c) maintenance consisting of feeding with a nutritionally stable canine diet   including meat and supplement when necessary
d) providing whatever training necessary to ensure this puppy's emotional/social stability (minimum completion of Puppy Kindergarten)
e) buyer will not have any puppy dipped in Mitaban or any other toxic substance for treatment related to transient Demodecosis unless under the approval of Breeder.
f) buyer will administer prescription drugs to puppy only as directed by licensed veterinarian.
g) buyer will keep breeder informed of any significant health, temperament or behavior problems encountered throughout the dogs life.

Purchaser is responsible for updated pictures of this puppy/dog at least twice in the first year approximately 6 mos. apart and once a year thereafter as long as dog/puppy resides at Purchaser's home.

Breeder is responsible for:

a) providing buyer with a healthy, sound, puppy/dog/bitch free of parasites and disease Breeder guarantees against infectious disease for a period of 14 days after pick up of puppy. The same applies to intestinal parasites.

b) providing a full refund or replacement under the following schedule should said puppy

1. develop heart ailment by age 2 (or later if it can be demonstrated that the condition is a congenital anomaly or existed previous to sale)
2. be diagnosed with Portal Systemic Shunt) dysfunction at any time in its life
3. develop Hip Dysplasia within 3 years
4. be diagnosed with bleeding disorders or other clearly inherited immuned mediated disorder
5. be diagnosed with any disorder clearly of an inherited or congenital nature as confirmed by a board certified licensed specialist of the disorder in question.

The above health guarantee will become void should buyer violate the terms of Buyer Responsibilities that are health/welfare related. This is a mutual agreement between Breeder and Purchaser. All terms and conditions of this are binding and non-negotiable. Should the terms of this agreement be violated, whether incidentally or deliberately, Breeder will pursue her options as stated in the Agreement to the fullest. Further should it become necessary to pursue legal action to fulfill terms of this agreement, Purchaser will be held liable for all legal fees and court costs.

Any placement costs, maintenance costs, boarding, medical and associated miscellaneous costs related to this puppy/dog will be the responsibility of Purchaser.

Liquidation damages in the amount of $3500.00 will be payable to Breeder by Purchaser in addition to the above costs and expenses.

By my signature I affirm that I have read, discussed and understood the terms and conditions of this agreement. Further, I agree to abide by the letter of the terms and conditions as well as the spirit of this agreement. I am aware of and fully understand the possible consequences of breaching this agreement. I sign this agreement of my own free will and without duress.

Signature
Purchaser_____

Date_____

Signature Breeder_____

Date_____

"From Cradle to Grave - Because First They Were My Pets, And Now They Are Yours"

NOTES:

1) The key points not to omit are the liquidation clause (monetary penalty), and the full explanation of the difference between Full and Limited Registration.
2) If deposits are taken on puppies, it is safest for buyer and seller to make the necessary modifications to paragraph #1 which will make this a receipt for the deposit. This way it is clear that a deposit was freely given on a puppy to be sold under the above terms and that having understood the terms, potential buyer gave a deposit.
3) You may include your own personal health guarantees and use this contract or any portion of it you may find helpful.
4) You may also include a section that specifies sex, date of birth, AKC litter registrations number, AKC registration number, sire and dam.

Contract contributed by Isabell Molina, owner of RingWise@MyList.net

Resources

No-Kill Shelters
Yorkie Clubs
Yorkie Rescues
Puppy Mill Information
Coat Handler Products
General Product Info
AKC Breed Standard

- An estimated 52 million dogs and 57 million cats live with U.S. families.
- **For every human born, 7 puppies and kittens are born.**
- One female cat and her offspring can produce 420,000 cats in 7 years.
- **One female dog and her offspring can produce 67,000 puppies in 6 years.**
- More than 12 million dogs and cats are euthanized in shelters each year.
- **As many as 25% of dogs entering shelters each year are purebreds.**
- Millions more are abandoned in rural and urban areas.
- **Approximately 61% of all dogs entering shelters are killed.**
- Approximately 75% of all cats entering shelters are killed.
- **It costs approximately $100 to capture, house, feed, and eventually kill each stray animal — a cost which you, the taxpayer, eventually pay.**

The above statistics used with permission from the 1996 Spay Day USA Participant Information Booklet published by the Doris Day Animal League located in Washington, D.C.

For an updated list of no-kill shelters, go online to www.fluffynet.com

Alabama
Greater Birmingham H S
1713 Lomb Avenue
Birmingham, AL 35208
205-780-7281
www.gbhs.org

Arizona
Arizona Humane Society
9226 North 13th Avenue
Phoenix, AZ 85021
Phone (602) 997 – 7585
www.flealess.org/azhumane.html

Humane Society of Southern AZ
3450 N. Kelvin Blvd.
Tucson, AZ 85716
(520) 327-6088
www.humane-so-arizona.org

California
All Creatures Animal Care
PO Box 3664
San Rafael, CA 94912
(415) 456-1941
www.swiftsite.com/allcreatures

Newport Beach Animal Shelter
2075 Newport Blvd.
Costa Mesa, CA (949) 644-3656

Pet Adoption Fund
7507 Deering Avenue
Canoga Park, CA 91303

Georgia

DeKalb Humane Society
5287 Covington Highway
Decatur, GA 30035-2202
(770) 593-1155

Illinois

Animal Welfare League
10305 Southwest Highway
Chicago Ridge, Illinois 60415
(708) 636-8586

Animal Welfare League
6224 South Wabash Ave.
Chicago, Illinois 60637
(312) 667-0088

Massachusetts

Buddy Dog Humane Society
151 Boston Post Road (Route 20)
Sudbury, MA 01776
(781) 237-4747
www.buddydoghs.com

Neponset Valley H. S.
152 North Main Street
Mansfield, MA 02048
508-261-9924

New England

H. S. of New England
24 Ferry Road
Nashua, NH 03064-8109
(603) 889-2275

New York

Animal Haven
35-22 Prince Street
Flushing, NY 11354
(718) 886-3683

Oklahoma

Pets & People H.S.
501 Ash

Yukon, OK 73099
(405) 350-PETS
www.petsandpeople.com

Texas

Humane Animal Rescue Team
PO Box 153293
Irving, TX 75015-3293
(214) 332-9535

Utah

Best Friends Animal Sanctuary
5001 Angel Canyon Drive
Kanab, UT 84741-5001
(435) 644-2001
www.bestfriends.org

Wisconsin

Tri-County Animal Shelter
PO Box 86
Green Lake, WI 54941
(920) 294-3042
www.puppyhome.com

SOS DOGS - Save our Small Dogs
Serving NJ, PA, DE and NY
8 Downing St.
Cherry Hill, NJ 08003-1519
609-424-3424
sosdogs@aol.com

YORKSHIRE TERRIER CLUBS (Y.T.C.s)—US

Y.T.C. of Greater Los Angeles
Shelly Ince
10907 E. Bella Vista Dr.
Scottsdale, AZ 85259
(602) 391-1788

Y.T.C. of Northern California
Kaye Strangeland
1121 S. Stelling Rd.
Cupertino, CA 95014
(408) 446-2008

The Rocky Mountain Y.T.C. (CO)
Marilyn Corwin
1504 Lucille Ct.
Northglenn, CO 80233
(303) 457-2806

Central Florida Y.T.C. (FL)
Suzette Heider
1058 Citrus Ave. NE
Palm Bay, FL 32905
(407) 725-8821

Y.T.C. of SE Michigan (MI)
Pat Lamia
19321 Bonkay
Clinton Twp, MI 48036
(810) 468-3549

Cyndi Campfield
451 Cedar St.
Jenkintown, PA 19046
(H): (215) 885-2612;
(W): (215) 885-1405

Twin Cities Area Y.T.C. (MN)
Marlene Dick
632 Lexington Pkwy. N.
St. Paul, MN 55104
(612) 489-2696

Watchung Mountains Y.T.C. (NJ)
Claire Pollitzer
Box 472/Quemby Mtn. Rd.
Great Meadows, NJ 07838
(908) 637-6326

Y.T.C. of Greater New York (NY)
Marilyn Koenig
665 Rt. 208
Gardiner, NY 12525
(914) 255-6549

Helen Stern
2057 Ford St.
Brooklyn, NY 11229
(718) 648-8557

Sharon Dykman
100 Good Hill Rd.
Oxford, CT 06478
(203) 888-3980

Delaware Valley Y.T.C. (PA)
Shirley A. Patterson
2 Chestnut Ct. - Star Rt.
Pottstown, PA 19464
(610) 469-6781

Bluebonnet Y.T.C. Rescue (TX)
Susan Griffin
2712 Dorrington
Dallas, TX 75228
(214) 320-9469

Y.T.C. of Greater Houston (TX)
Barbara Gilless
10115 Spring Place Dr.
Houston, TX 77070
(713) 894-5597

YORKSHIRE TERRIER CLUBS—INTERNATIONAL

FRANCE
Mme. Liliane Richard
Club Français du Terrier du
Yorkshire
1, rue Montespan
91000 EVRY
01 69 36 43 33

ENGLAND
The Yorkshire Terrier Club
Secretary, Hazel Hammersley
4, Stookes Way
Yateley, Hampshire GU46 6YY
01 252 871 238

Northern Counties
Secretary, Mrs. M. Eades
8 Sunnyvale Mount
South Elmsall, West Yorkshire
WF9 2AX
01 977 643 824

Scotland
Secretary, Mrs. I.L. Rae
5/1 Calder Grove
Sighthill, Edinburgh EH11 4NB
01 131 453 2870

Cheshire & New Wales
Secretary, Mrs. J Bebbington
70 Middlewick Street
Crewe, Cheshire CW1 4DG

South Wales
Secretary, Mr. T. Evans
Plot 2 Raven Court Hillside Terrace
Gelli, Rhondda, Mid Glamorgan
CF41 7UH
01 443 431 052

Eastern Counties
Secretary, Mrs. C. Wilson
Mill Villa
Over, Cambs C84 5PP
012 954 230 742

South Western
Secretary, Mrs. J. Drake
1 Station Road
Kingswood, Bristol, Avon BS15 4PG
01 272 601 592

Lincoln & Humberside
Secretary, Mr.R. Terry
The Bungalow, Holton-cum-Beckering
Market Rasen, Lincolnshire LN8 5NG
01 673 858 044

Ulster
Secretary, Mrs. C. Wood
21 Carnhill Avenue
Carnmoney, Newton Abbey, Belfast
BT36 6LE Northern Ireland
01 232 841 484

Midland
Secretary, Mrs. J. Bradley
107 Lanchester Road

Kings Norton, Birmingham
B38 9AG

SWITZERLAND
Schweizerischer YTC (SYC)
Eidgenössisch bewilligt und
eingetragener Verein
Sekretariat Ankegässli 14
CH-8956
Killwangen Switzerland
056 401 59 83
syc@euromail.com

SPAIN
Club Español del Yorkshire
Terrier
Avícola del Jarama 8 Ctra.
Chinchón km. 3.200 28500
Arganda del Rey Madrid
91 871 94 73

The Meaning of Rescue

Now that I'm home, bathed, settled and fed,
All nicely tucked in my warm new bed,
I'd like to open my baggage
Lest I forget,
There is so much to carry,
So much to regret.
Hmm.. yes, there it is, right on the top,
Let's unpack Loneliness, Heartache and Loss,
And there by my leash hides Fear and Shame.
As I look on these things I tried so hard to leave,
I still have to unpack my baggage called Pain.
I loved them, the others, the ones who left me,
But I wasn't good enough for they didn't want me.
Will you add to my baggage?
Will you help me unpack?
Or will you just look at my things
And take me right back?
Do you have the time to help me unpack,
To put away my baggage,
To never repack?
I pray that you do, I'm so tired you see,
But I do come with baggage.
Will you still want me?

—unknown

RESCUE—US /INTERNATIONAL

Online www.petfinder.org

NATIONAL
Y.T.C. of America National
Rescue National Chairman:
Mary Elizabeth Dugmore
Chapmansboro, TN
(615) 746-4401
dugmore@bellsouth.net
Has regional rescue list
www.yorkshireterrierrescue.com

AKC Companion Animal
Recovery 5580 Centerview
Drive, Suite 250 Raleigh, NC

27604-3394
(800) 252-7894
fax: (919) 233-1290
found@akc.org

Tatoo-A-Pet
Lost Pet Hot Line: 954-581-0079
(24 hours/day)
Office: 954-581-5834
Ft. Lauderdale, FL
www.tattoo-a-pet.com.

Florida
Melissa Harrison
Ft.Myers,FL

harrison@tfn.net

Suzette Heider
1058 Citrus Avenue NE
Palm Bay, FL 32905

Ruth Ward
Panama City,FL
(850)785-0614
rustco@worldnet.att.net

Michigan
Marlene Boufflers
Small Dog Rescue League
PO Box 433
Mayville, MI 48744
Fax: 517-761-7062
smalldogs@centuryinter.net

New Jersey
Jane Bonkoski
Salem County,NJ
bonkoski@jnlk.com

Pennsylvania
Marilyn Faughner
Sinking Spring,PA
(610)670-2183
faughner@aol.com

Utah
Deborah Nendell
3862 South Sennie Dr.
Magna, UT 84044
(H): 801-252-1729
(W): 801-567-8240
DebSamPep@aol.com

ENGLAND
Beryl Evans
23 Starling Way
Bedford MK41 7HW
01 234 262 515

Elaine Stuart
Adelaine Boarding Kennels

Rose Cottage, Boat Lane
Stoneyford, Notts NG16 5PR
01 773 768 071

Puppy Mills

A puppy mill is the starting point of a product that is mass-produced and destined for the retail industry...via wholesale channels. Puppy mills don't have to be dirty, they don't have to be illegal, they don't have to have sick and dying dogs...they just have to produce dogs for the wholesale dog industry. [from nopuppymills.com web site]

NoPuppyMills.com is not an organization. It is one brave woman (Kim Townsend) maintaining a web site designed to provide information on the wholesale dog industry in America and the sad and despicable conditions associated with puppy mills. Visit her web site at

www.nopuppymills.com

If you would like to contribute to NoPuppyMills.com, you can send contributions to:

NoPuppyMills.com
PO Box 922
Ft. Leonard Wood, MO 65473

Your contribution will be acknowledged with a receipt (and a Thank You!).

A Story Of Someone Who Attended A Dog Auction

The place was much as I expected. Converted chicken houses and mobile homes were the only homes these dogs knew. The stench was incredible. It appeared that someone had tried to clean the place before the sale. You could see that the large, concrete dog pens were still wet, and although there were still many piles of feces, you could tell it had been much worse. The pores of the concrete were filled with feces, and instead of a white or grey color that you normally see on concrete, it was brown. The dogs that had white paws were clear indicators of the filth they lived in. paws covered halfway up with feces and urine.

The smaller cages were stacked, two-story buildings and they wouldn't let me in them. The children of the man who was running the auction would take metal pipes and poke at the dogs in the cages so that they could be grabbed and taken to the auction table. These dogs were so terrified by being poked that they would run to the inside of the cage, only to be grabbed.

One stacked wire cage held a golden retriever and her four puppies—about four weeks old. The golden and all the puppies were on a wire floored cage about the same size as the mother. There wasn't even a place for the puppies to lie and they had to lie on top of the mother—that or be laid on by their own mother.

I did bid on a dachshund that was blind. I saw her in one of the cages and you could tell that she knew someone was there. She bumped into all sides of the cage before she found my waiting finger. I think she thought it was food because she would lick and bite on it. The cage wire was very tiny and I couldn't fit more than a finger through it, but I would have tried to force my whole body through it if I knew I could just hold and love this dog.

At one point, she turned around and I saw that there was a large matted clump of hair hanging from her mouth. It reminded me of the hair you clean from the drain of your bathtub. Tangled in her teeth, I could only imagine how long it had been there. She pawed at it every few seconds to try and remove it, but only after I managed to get my finger in just enough to pull on it, after several tries, did I finally dislodge it. Despite being about eight months old and blind, she sold for $150. I walked out with tears in my eyes. How I wish I was rich!

I met a news crew down the road from the auction location and I poured my heart out to them. It looks like it might actually do some good on a national level soon.

Dog auctions are legal and we won't stop them, but the people that attend them and anyone who loves animals should know where these pet shop puppies come from.

STOP PUPPY MILLS—
DON'T BUY FROM PET STORES!

COAT HANDLER PRODUCTS

COAT HANDLER CONDITIONER CONCENTRATE:
A "leave in" conditioner that is a detangler, antistatic, and fragrance all-in-one product. Does NOT soften coats or make them oily since it has no oil, silicone, or lanolin in it. Enhances natural shine and keeps the animal clean longer.

COAT HANDLER GROOMER'S 15 FOR 1 SHAMPOO CONCENTRATE:
Dilutes easily, rinses quickly and completely. Leaves no residue to build up. It is cosmetic grade (human quality) and very mild. Will get rid of the "chemical buildup" of other products. Restores shine and colors that the animals had as youngsters since the best colors are in the genes, not in bottles. It may be used as often as once a month and not dry out a coat.

COAT HANDLER PREMIUM 5 TO 1 SHAMPOO CONCENTRATE:
Extremely mild and hypoallergenic (contains no fragrance). Can be used daily without stripping color or drying skin or coat. It is wonderful for once-a-week (high maintenance) dogs or soft coats.

SENSATIONAL DETANGLER SPRAY
A fabulous finishing spray, equally effective on wet or dry coats. It works great on cats as well as dogs and totally eliminates static. Contains no silicone, oil, or alcohol to create buildup or cause skin irritations. Does not "lay coat down" or make it appear oily.

THE SKIN WORKS
A greaseless, fragrance-free cream that heals "hot spots," clipper burns, irritations, insect bites and helps with yeast infections. It soothes pain, reduces swelling and inflammation, softens callouses, and moisturizes dry skin. Contains no steroids and is non-toxic.

ODOR HANDLER
A bio-degradable, non-toxic crystalline powder for use in removing odors (not covering up with a sticky sweet smell). Contains powerful ingredients that are safe for most surfaces, fabrics, and colors. As a carpet and upholstery cleaner, it deodorizes, effectively removes stains, and brightens colors. Non-toxic and environmentally safe.

SENPROCO INC./COATHANDLER: 800-748-1777

Products & Miscellaneous Yorkie Information

Azmira Holistic Animal Care
2100 North Wilmot Road Suite 109
Tucson, AZ 85712
(800)497-5665
Makers of Azmira natural pet foods and supplements

Natura Pet Products
(800) 532-7261
www.naturapet.com
Makers of California Natural pet food and other natural foods

Sherpa's Pet Trading Company
135 East 55th Street
New York, New York 10022
TEL: (800) 743-7723 • (212) 838-9837 • (212) 308-1187 (fax)
Makers of the Sherpa lightweight, airline-approved pet carrier

Senproco Inc.
(800) 748-1777 • (605) 373-1166 fax
Makers of Coat Handler products
www.coathandler.com

Citronella Collar
UPCO Catalog: (800) 254-8726 (order line) • (816) 233-9696 (fax)

Wysong
422 Larkfield Center #312
Santa Rosa, CA 95403
(707) 545-8394 • (707)-546-0843 (fax)
www.docsez.com
(pet foods and natural supplements)

Pro Vet Supply
Upland, CA
(909) 981-9313
makers of exercise pens; custom sizes and styles available

- www.yorkiehouse.com: Great site for Yorkie products
- www.shooterdog.com: Great site for links to various Yorkie information
- www2.hawaii.edu/~anzenber/iyc.htm: International Yorkie chat

AOL message board on Yorkshire Terriers. Keyword: dog & select breed.

AKC BREED STANDARD
YORKSHIRE TERRIER

General Appearance: That of a long-haired toy terrier whose blue and tan coat is parted on the face and from the base of the skull to the end of the tail and hangs evenly and quite straight down each side of the body. The body is neat, compact, and well proportioned. The dog's high head carriage and confident manner should give the appearance of vigor and self-importance.

Head: Small and rather flat on top, the skull not too prominent or round, the muzzle not too long, with the bite neither undershot nor overshot and teeth sound. Either scissors bite or level bite is acceptable. The nose is black. Eyes are medium in size and not too prominent; dark in color and sparkling with a sharp intelligent expression. Eye rims are dark. Ears are small, V-shaped, carried erect and set not too far apart.

Body: Well proportioned and very compact. The back is rather short, the back line level, with height at shoulder the same as at the rump.

Weight: Must not exceed seven pounds.

Legs and Feet: Forelegs should be straight, elbows neither in nor out. Hind legs straight when viewed from behind, but stifles are moderately bent when viewed from the sides. Feet are round with black toenails. Dewclaws, if any, are generally removed from the hind legs. Dewclaws on the forelegs may be removed.

Tail: Docked to a medium length and carried higher than the level of the back.

Coat: Quality, texture and quantity of coat are of prime importance. Hair is glossy, fine and silky in texture. Coat on the body is moderately long and perfectly straight (not wavy). It may be trimmed to floor length to give ease of movement and a neater appearance, if desired. The fall on the head is long, tied with one bow in center of head or parted in the middle and tied with two bows. Hair on muzzle is very long. Hair should be trimmed short on tips of ears and may be trimmed on feet to give them a neat appearance.

Colors: Puppies are born black and tan and are normally darker in body color, showing intermingling of black hair in the tan until they are matured. Color of hair on body and richness of tan on head and legs are of prime importance in adult dogs, to which the following color requirements apply:

> **Blue**: Is a dark steel-blue, not a silver-blue and not mingled with fawn, bronzy or black hairs.
>
> **Tan**: All tan hair is darker at the roots than in the middle, shading to still lighter tan at the tips. There should be no sooty or black hair intermingled with any of the tan.
>
> **Color on Body**: The blue extends over the body from the back of the neck to the root of the tail. Hair on tail is a darker blue, especially at end of tail.
>
> **Headfall**: A rich golden tan, deeper in color at sides of head, at ear roots and on the muzzle, with ears a deep rich tan. Tan color should not extend down on back of neck.
>
> **Chest and Legs**: A bright rich tan, not extending above the elbow on the forelegs nor above the stifle

Index

NOTES AND SOURCES

E Friedmann, SA Thomas: Pet Ownership, social support and one year survival after myocardial infarction in the Cardiac Arrhythmia Suppression Trial, *American Journal of Cardiology*, 1995. (chapter 1)

James Serpell PhD: Beneficial effects of pet ownership on some aspects of human health & behaviour, *Journal of Royal Science of Medicine*, Volume 84, December 1991. (chapter 1)

*****

Carlson, Delbert, D.V.M., and Giffin, James, M.D., *Dog Owner's Home Veterinary Handbook*. Howell Book House: New York, NY, 1992. (new edition available Nov. 99)

Fodor's, *On the Road With Your Pet*. New York, NY: Fodor's Travel Publications, 1998.

Hunsicker, Christine, ed., *A Dog's World: True Stories of Man's Best Friend on the Road*. Traveler's Tales, Inc.: San Francisco, CA, 1998.

Sandy Lemire has 25 years experience in breeding, raising, and showing toy dogs, especially Yorkshire Terriers, Toy Poodles and Shih Tzus. She is widely published in *Yorkshire Terrier Magazine*, *Yorkshire Terrier Annual*, various dog magazines, and holistic pet care newsletters and magazines. She developed Coat Handler shampoos, conditioners, and other products that are sold internationally with great success in maintaining show quality coats for pets and show dogs alike.

Her passion for the health and nurturing of the Toy Dog led her to found the "Culture Program" as a means of defining health-related breeding techniques. Her studies of the science involved in these techniques led to periodic lectures and articles for breed professionals regarding zoonotic diseases and other breed-related subjects. Ms. Lemire's first book, *Form, Function & Fancy* covers these topics. Her research also led to the launching of her Coat Handler grooming products. These well-known products have grown since 1985 to form the basis of two international corporations.

Sandy lives in Durango, CO with five Yorkies and her honey, Gary.